JAMES M. EFIRD

*For
Elaine
Best Wishes
+
Blessings
James M. Efird*

# Left
# Behind?

WHAT THE BIBLE REALLY SAYS
ABOUT THE END TIMES

Smyth & Helwys Publishing, Inc.
6316 Peake Road
Macon, Georgia 31210-3960
1-800-747-3016
©2006 by Smyth & Helwys Publishing

The paper used in this publication meets the minimum requirements of
American National Standard for Information Sciences—
Permanence of Paper for Printed Library Materials.
ANSI Z39.48–1984. (alk. paper)

*Library of Congress Cataloging-in-Publication Data*

Efird, James M.
Left behind? : what the Bible really says about the end times /
by James M. Efird.
p. cm.
Includes bibliographical references (p.      ) and index.
ISBN 1-57312-461-3 (pbk. : alk. paper)
1. Eschatology—Biblical teaching.
2. Plymouth Brethren—Doctrines.
3. Bible—Criticism, interpretation, etc.
I. Title.
BS680.E8E45 2006
236'.9--dc22

2005032227

# CONTENTS

# DEDICATION

*For Vivian, for whom I am deeply grateful*

# ACKNOWLEDGMENTS

There are numerous people to whom I owe a great deal of gratitude for this work. First of all, I want to thank Keith Gammons and the people at Smyth & Helwys Publishing for asking me to do a revision of this earlier book (previously titled *End-Times: Rapture, Antichrist, Millenium*) and for their unending patience in waiting for its completion. There have been many delays, and they have been gracious and understanding in granting me more time to complete the project.

Further, two of my best friends have contributed greatly to this endeavor. Mr. Bill Sullivan, of Trinity, North Carolina, who is one of the most learned biblical laypeople I have ever encountered, has been gracious in talking with me and pointing me in directions I might not have gone on my own. Many thanks to him. Secondly, I thank my former student and dear friend Rev. Steve Braswell, who is senior pastor at Graham Presbyterian Church in Graham, North Carolina. Steve was one of the best students I taught among many in my forty-seven years at Duke Divinity School. He has updated and compiled the new bibliography for this revised edition and has made valuable suggestions.

I am indebted to both of these men. Futher, I would like to express my deep appreciation to Ms. Andrea Bridges for her painstaking work in typing the manuscript, parts of it more than once!

Finally, I am always grateful to my dear wife Vivian, who always has encouraged and supported my work in several areas, especially in writing. She is a constant source of light and joy for me. Since I shall probably not write another book, I want this last one to be dedicated to her.

# INTRODUCTION

The first edition of this book was conceived, written, and published in anticipation of the expected fervor over the coming of the year 1988 and subsequently the turn of the millennium, which came to be known as the Y2K phenomenon. The fervor happened, but the "end times" as some expected did not occur.

In the time between 1988 and the present, other phenomena relating to end times have appeared, but the one causing the most commotion and generating the most controversy is the *Left Behind* series by Tim LaHaye and Jerry Jenkins. The twelve volumes of this series have sold more than 62 million copies worldwide. A "prequel" and "sequel" to the series are planned, as well as additional books by LaHaye. At least three movies have been made from the early volumes, and different approaches teaching the basic concepts of the books have been devised for children, teenagers, and others.

Since this series has been and continues to be pervasive in our culture, it was determined that my original book needed an update with special reference to the newer movement pertaining to end times. When I wrote the first edition, the most prominent group advocating that the biblical "code" had been broken and that the "end times" were about to begin was the "Darbyists," followers of the system of interpretation set forth in 1829 by a young Irishman named John Nelson Darby. His theological system of interpreting Scripture, called *dispensationalism*, is not our concern; instead, we will focus on his eschatological system. And recently, adherents of this system have espoused many new ideas, known as "progressive dispensationalism."

It is not the purpose of this short volume to enter into an analysis of the entire system. Rather, the focus is on the end-times eschatology espoused and advocated by the Darbyists. Even to this day, the basic "end-times grid" of the Darbyists and their fellow travelers remains essentially the same.

Perhaps no single issue or topic strikes more fear into the hearts of church people, engenders more heated debate, or brings out a bigger and more interested crowd than that of the end times, popularly known as "the Second Coming." This concept centers on the early church belief that Jesus would return soon, within the people's lifetimes, to fulfill the work of the kingdom of God that was inaugurated during Jesus' earthly ministry. This belief is known in scholarly circles as the *Parousia*, the "presence" or "coming" of Jesus. Even though the timing of the Parousia turned out to be erroneous, the idea has persisted throughout the centuries of church history and has garnered a considerable amount of attention.

Many people through the years held to the belief that Jesus was to return and espoused many different theories in an attempt to explain exactly what would happen when he did. A large number of these theories began in the nineteenth century, and they are still prevalent in some circles today. The most well known of these systems is popularly called "Bible prophecy" and centers on "end-of-the-world" speculation. The more sophisticated system from which this theology derives is technically known as dispensationalism.

As with any theological system, the adherents of dispensationalism argue many different ideas. It is difficult to find two dispensational schemes with regard to the end times that agree at all points. However, several basic key concepts frequently appear in the writings of this particular school of interpretation. They can be loosely assigned to three general categories: rapture, antichrist, and millennium. This book examines these three areas and certain attendant ideas to ascertain whether dispensationalism has been true to the biblical text.

The best approach to this task appears to be to introduce the reader to a brief history of the origins and development of the system. Sometimes knowing the origins and presuppositions of a theology can assist one in evaluating the teachings and components of the system. After this brief examination of the history and background of the dispensational system, the three key elements of the end-times teaching will be discussed. As mentioned already, these are rapture, antichrist, and millennium. The key passages used for support of the dispensational teachings will be examined within their contexts in the biblical writings to ascertain whether they have been properly understood and correctly interpreted.

It must be pointed out that only the most basic of the passages will be analyzed here. Space does not allow for a full examination of every text used in support of the system. The proponents of dispensationalism attempt to support their interpretation of certain passages by appealing to many other verses or pieces of verses drawn out of context from various places in the biblical accounts. All of these cannot be examined, partly because different Scripture texts appeal to different groups, and the groups do not always agree on certain aspects of the system. The key elements are essentially the same, however, and we will examine them in this book.

It must be noted that while the discussion will focus on the dispensational system, especially as it relates to end-times teaching, the reader may recognize certain other familiar ideas and teachings. This is because the dispensational system of interpretation has enjoyed wide coverage, and its teachings have influenced other groups such as those involved in the *Left Behind* phenomenon and other systems of interpretation. In short, members of other systems either knowingly or unknowingly have appropriated certain parts of the dispensational system without being devotees of the entire system. We will focus on the dispensational system and on its elements that have become part of other ideologies.

A bibliography is provided at the conclusion of the analysis to encourage further investigation of the various approaches and ideas. Some critics of the system have argued that it is wrong because it is relatively new, having been around for only about 175 years. Others argue against it because they believe it has been a divisive factor in the church since its inception, and still others question the background and leadership of the movement. The more responsible advocates of the dispensational system argue that one should not reject a teaching simply because it is new, because it has been a divisive force in the church, or because it has come from questionable backgrounds. In this contention they are absolutely correct, and it is not fair to the proponents of dispensationalism (or any other theological system) to judge it on the basis of any criterion other than that the teaching is true to the biblical texts. No theology, system, or individual teaching should be called biblical if it does not reflect the proper meaning the original inspired authors intended. Further, no teaching should be understood as biblical unless it is first understood as it was by the original hearers/readers. The purpose of this book is to examine the key teachings of dispensationalism against the biblical passages its advocates use as support. We will try to ascertain if the ideas of rapture, antichrist, and millennium are indeed presented in the biblical texts as the dispensationalists argue.

# CHAPTER ONE

# A Brief Sketch of Dispensationalism

The system of biblical interpretation known by its proponents as "Bible prophecy" is well known. The system's devotees have done an excellent job of making their interpretation easily accessible to laypeople in a form that is understandable, simply described, and confidently propounded. There are numerous characteristics of this system, known properly as *dispensationalism*, most notably the emphasis upon the end times and the events that are to constitute and accompany that momentous occasion. Of these events, perhaps the three most well known are the rapture, the antichrist, and the millennium.

Contrary to what many people have thought, this system of interpretation has not been around since the time of Jesus and the New Testament church. It is only about 175 years old, and yet it has exercised a tremendous but disproportionate amount of influence in its short existence. Dispensational spokespeople have argued correctly that the relative newness of their ideas does not automatically make them invalid. What makes a system valid or invalid is whether the proponents of that system and its teachings have understood and interpreted the Bible correctly.

Generally speaking, in order to understand and interpret the Bible properly a person must come to the biblical writings with one primary concern in mind: _What did the original author(s) intend in their inspired writing, and how did the original readers/hearers understand that message?_ In order to interpret the biblical books correctly, therefore, modern readers must attempt as much as possible to place themselves in the time and context when the book originally appeared. To do this requires painstaking work, but without the effort the modern interpreter cannot truly understand the Scriptures. The biblical teachings about eschatology, i.e., "the study of the end," must be understood in such a manner. What, then, was the setting for the New Testament teachings about eschatology?

## Parousia

Since the ascension of Jesus (perhaps even before), members of the Christian church have been curious about Jesus' return, the conclusion of history, and the final victory of God's work begun in Christ. Of greatest concern is _when_ these events will occur. The early church of Peter and Paul believed that the _Parousia_ (the New Testament term for Jesus' return) would occur within their lifetime. In fact, some of Paul's advice given in response to his churches' questions was based on the sincere belief that they were living in the last age and generation of history. A sense of urgency is evident in the preaching of the early church.

After AD 70, however, with the destruction of the temple in Jerusalem and the realization that the church was entering into a second (and in some cases even a third) generation, it became clear that Jesus was not going to return within the originally expected time period. This was an embarrassment to these people and caused many to rethink the issue. In fact, almost all of the New Testament books written after AD 70 deal in some way with the disappointment and embarrassment over the delay in the Parousia.

One can read Ephesians, which talks about the "ages" to come and future "generations." The author does not seem to mention the Parousia, however. In Matthew's Gospel, chapters 24–25 address a "delay" and conclude with a series of four parables that deal with how those left to work in the absence of a superior should react and behave when the superior's return is delayed. Matthew's point to the church is fairly obvious. Jesus has been delayed in returning; in spite of that, Matthew instructs us to continue doing what we were commanded to do in the interim period, no matter how long it lasts. Of course, the Gospel concludes with the Great Commission and Jesus' promise to be with them until "the end of the age." There is no indication of how long that might be.

Chronologically, the letter known as 2 Peter is the last of the canonical New Testament writings. The author explains that there has been a delay, but God will bring the world to an end when God decides to do so. No timetable is set!

The church could have simply given up the entire concept of the Parousia, but instead reaffirmed its certainty that God's work begun in Jesus would someday be brought to completion. The temptation, however, to attempt to set a date for the end times did not go away. In the late second century and beyond, many speculated about this issue. The return of Jesus was linked to the concept of the 1,000-year reign of Jesus with the saints in Revelation 20. There was no absolute consensus, but the basic idea was that the millennial kingdom had already begun—it was the church in the world now. After 1,000 years, Jesus would return and conclude God's work. This school of thought is called post-millennialism, i.e., Jesus returns after the 1,000-year reign.

One can image the anxiety felt by people living in the 990s (one might say there was a Y1K problem!). But the year 1000 came and went, as did 1100 and 1200. At that point, most believed the number 1,000 to be symbolic and felt that after that period of time, God would send Jesus back.

As one recalls from the study of the history of the church, many changes were taking place—the Reformation and the many alternatives to the church's polity and theology that arose after the Reformation. There were also social and economic upheavals in the 1700s and 1800s due to the Industrial Revolution and political revolutions, particularly in the Western world. It would have been almost impossible not to think changes were about to take place in the church and in its teachings.

## Apocalyptic

Most of the New Testament teachings about the return of Christ were presented in a literary style known as *apocalyptic*. This movement, which began in postexilic Judaism (c. 300–200 BC), was at first a "thought pattern" that developed a literary style to serve as a vehicle for speaking to persecuted people. At base, the apocalyptic ideology held that a cosmic battle between the forces of good and the forces of evil was taking place in the world. Since the earth is part of the cosmic order, the battle also rages within human history, and people are called upon to ally themselves with one side or the other. In apocalyptic literature, there is little room for "gray" areas. The battle, it was believed, would be long and hard. There were times when good had the upper hand; there were times when the two sides were nearly "even"; but there were also times when evil had the upper hand, and in such situations those on the side of good suffered and were persecuted.

Even though it was thought that there would be a final end to all this conflict and that good would ultimately triumph over evil, the Hebrew concept of history kept the people from thinking of only one great conflict at the "end." The idea of Jewish apocalyptic writings centered on "ages," specifically a present age that had come under the domination of the forces of evil and could only be redeemed by the intervention of God. God alone could take away the persecution and restore the people to a "normal" life. This led to the idea of a two-age system in Jewish thought, a present age under the dominion of the forces of evil and a soon-to-come new age in which the persecution would be removed. The main point to remember is that history continues to move along, and in the course of events a new period of evil may be born, thus repeating the cycle again.

One can readily ascertain that such thinking was especially appealing in periods of persecution or "hard times." Since the Jewish community in Palestine had returned from exile in Babylon in 538 BC, their lot had been anything but good. They were politically powerless, economically poor, and militarily defenseless. For many years they languished in such a situation, vulnerable to any who decided to come into their area and loot or pillage. It is no wonder that apocalyptic thinking became part of the people's mind-set during this stage of their existence. To facilitate the dissemination of these ideas, a literary style was created, characterized by the use of strange symbols and images. For people who were a part of that culture and time, these symbols and images were readily recognizable, much in the same way as people today recognize the meaning of political cartoons. No one has to explain the grotesque figures and images to us; most people know their intent because they employ a literary device common to our culture and time.

In apocalyptic symbolism, beasts stood for nations; heads on beasts represented rulers; numbers had specific but symbolic meanings; so did colors. In any apocalyptic work (as with any biblical book), the interpreter must know something about the historical setting in which the book was written so as to interpret the book as the inspired author intended it to be understood and to listen to the text as one of those for whom the book was originally written. Only by doing this can the interpreter truly understand the meaning of a biblical text, especially an apocalyptic text. The modern interpreter must be extremely careful not to read into the text ideas that were not in the original setting and that would not have been in the minds of the original author and the original hearers/readers. (For examples of careful interpretation, see the reputable commentaries and studies on biblical books, especially Daniel and Revelation, which are listed in the bibliography at the conclusion of this book.)

Apocalyptic ideas and symbolism can be found in numerous parts of the New Testament, and the last six chapters of the book of Daniel (7–12) are apocalyptic. The most thoroughly apocalyptic book in the Bible, however, is the book of Revelation, also known as the "Apocalypse." This type of thinking and writing flourished from about 200 BC–AD 100, but after that time the movement ceased. The Christian church entered into the Gentile, Greco-Roman world, which did not understand apocalyptic writing. The Jewish community, which was being expelled from Jerusalem and Palestine during this period, also gave up apocalyptic writing and thinking, partly because of the strong apocalyptic emphasis of the early Christian movement. In those days there were no printing presses or storage places to keep alive these literary products; thus, apocalyptic writing soon disappeared from the scene and with it the key to understanding the phenomenon.

The early Christians believed strongly that Jesus was going to return *soon*, in their generation, to consummate the kingdom of God that he had inaugurated during his earthly ministry. When this did not occur quickly, many still looked forward to Jesus' return. In attempting to determine when this might take place, many church fathers looked to Revelation and other apocalyptic passages for guidance. One of the passages on which they focused was the "millennium" section of Revelation 20 (20:4-6). This portion of Scripture speaks about a 1,000-year reign of the saints with Christ, thus the designation *millennium.*

By this time the understanding of apocalyptic thought and literature had nearly vanished, causing the church fathers much anguish in attempting to understand Revelation correctly. Partly because they did not feel comfortable with the interpretation of the book and partly because some groups used the teachings wrongly and disturbed many of the faithful, numerous church leaders felt that Revelation should not become part of the New Testament canon. By the end of the fourth century AD, however, the canon had been basically accepted and included Revelation.

It had also become clear by this time that the return of Jesus had at least been postponed until the indefinite future. This made the 1,000-year passage more attractive to those who speculated about these matters. Soon the overwhelming opinion of church leaders was that the presence of the church in the world was in fact the millennium and that after 1,000 years, Jesus would return to consummate the kingdom. (Since Jesus was to return *after* the 1,000 years, this idea was eventually known as *post*millennialism.) As time passed and the year AD 1000 approached, people grew apprehensive and talked about the return of Jesus. As the date came and went, however, naturally a reinterpretation occurred. Many held that the 1,000 years was a symbolic period of time and that Jesus would return at the end of that time frame, still basically retaining a postmillennial interpretation.

Others began to speculate that since 1,000 years was such a specific figure, perhaps the period of time had not yet begun, and in fact would not begin until after Jesus returned. This idea began to develop and reached its peak in the nineteenth century. The idea that Jesus was to return *before* the millennium came to be known as "*pre*millennialism." Couple this situation with growing speculation about who the "antichrist" might be, and one has the beginnings of a potential scenario in which speculation about "time, place, and characters" could develop rather dramatically.

## Questions for Study and Discussion

1. Do you think it is important to know the history of a popular fad or craze? Would you consider the "end-times" phenomenon a fad among some people? Have you ever read literature related to the "end-times" phenomenon? How seriously did you take it?

2. Do you think it is important to know the context of a particular verse or verses from a biblical book? Can reading Scripture out of context make a significant difference in what it means? Can you give examples of interpreting a verse or passage apart from its original background text?

3. Do you think we sometimes accept certain ideas as "biblical" without understanding their origins? Can you give examples?

4. Why do you think so many people accept ideas about the end times as scriptural and defend them vigorously?

5. What do you think about the authority of Scripture? What is the church's responsibility in helping people interpret the Bible?

6. Can you define "dispensationalism"? Do you agree with any of its components?

CHAPTER 2

# A Brief Sketch of Darbyism

In order to understand the setting that gave rise to the system of interpretation with such a wide dissemination today, the reader must recall the kind of world extant in the late eighteenth and nineteenth centuries. There was political upheaval, e.g., the revolution of the American colonists, the rise and fall of Napoleon, revolutions all over Europe, political changes in Great Britain; there was social unrest; and, of course, there was the Industrial Revolution with its economic impact on the scene followed by differing types of philosophies and ideologies that attempted to make sense of all the confusion. Not to be ignored was the work of the scientists, especially Charles Darwin and his associates with their shocking doctrine of evolution. Space does not permit even a partial listing of all the mind-boggling, shattering changes that occurred in those years. They were truly apocalyptic times in which people of sensitivity tried to make sense of the chaos that swirled around them.

Many people came to believe that the end times had drawn close. They had grown disillusioned with the established churches, especially in Great Britain. "Cell" groups began to meet apart from normal church functions for prayer and the study of Scripture. Most of the people involved with these groups were disappointed and disillusioned with the church structure, leadership, and doctrine. From these groups emerged a movement known as the Plymouth Brethren.

## John Nelson Darby and the Darbyists

At this point it is necessary to begin to concentrate on a single individual who was closely associated with the Plymouth Brethren movement and whose name is, for some, synonymous with it (even though he did not begin the phenomenon). In 1800 an Irish child who would leave his imprint on the history of the church in many lands was born in London. His name was John Nelson Darby. This young man was brilliant and a tireless worker. At first he studied law but soon became disillusioned with the "law" and subsequently studied for the priesthood of the Church of England (Anglican). He was ordained and took an appointment in Dublin. In 1827 he sustained an injury to his leg that required surgery and an extended period of convalescence. During his recovery, he had a religious experience that served to reinforce his growing disillusionment with the established church. He never tired of saying that the church was "in ruins."

Because of this disenchantment with the established church, Darby became associated with the "cell" groups that met apart from regular church activities. So strongly did he feel an affiliation with these groups that he renounced his ordination and became the major figure in the Plymouth Brethren movement. The emphasis in this group and with Darby was upon the interpretation of the Scriptures.

Through his study of the biblical books, Darby began to construct a "theology" that later grew into a full-blown system. Many of the ideas now held by proponents of that system were Darby's, supplemented by those of other people attracted to this type of interpretation. The major components of the system, however, were set into place by Darby and his followers, beginning about 1829.

First of all, Darby felt that the formal established church was basically corrupt and therefore useless. Because of the uncertainties of the time, the apocalyptic portions of the Bible so appealed to him that he became preoccupied with the return of Jesus and the events surrounding the end times. Darby (and his followers today) believed that the biblical teachings must be understood literally. When this was not always possible, the accepted procedure was to take the meaning of the text as its "normal" or "plain" meaning. Of course, Darby and his followers determined which of the approaches was appropriate in any given passage and decided what the "normal" or "plain" meaning was.

Because Darby and his followers became so preoccupied with end times, the entire system came to be understood as "Bible prophecy" pointing throughout to the end. Prophecy to this group was always "a prediction of the future." Closely related to this idea, and in a sense evolving from it, is one of the basic tenets of the system, namely that God has two plans and two different groups of people to carry out God's purposes. The two groups are: (1) Israel (meaning the Jewish nation of Israel) and (2) the church. Israel is God's earthly kingdom, and the church is only an afterthought, a "parenthesis," in God's dealing with the world that resulted when the Jewish nation rejected Jesus as its Messiah.

One of the primary reasons for this idea came from a misunderstanding of Old Testament history and a misinterpretation of certain prophetic passages. When the nation of Judah fell to the Babylonians in 586 BC—the city of Jerusalem sacked and destroyed and the people carried off into exile in Babylonia—the prophets told them to hold fast, that they would ultimately be restored to the land and be made a nation again. For those who study the prophetic books carefully, it is clear that most of the prophetic oracles are poetic. In almost any culture, poetry is not intended to be taken with an absolutely literal meaning. This was also true in ancient times with the Hebrew people. Many of the prophetic oracles pertaining to the restoration of the Jewish people in the land of Judah and their development into a nation were poetic. Therefore, to hold these teachings to an absolute literalism in every word would be an imposition on the materials of a meaning or meanings not originally intended by the prophets.

Darby and his devotees, however, understood this as "prophecy" that has never been fulfilled. Since God's word is absolute truth, they hold that this prediction must come to pass or else God's word is wrong. The problem with such an interpretation is that is does not understand poetry properly, nor does it admit that the prophecy was fulfilled! In 538 BC the Hebrew people in Babylon were told that they could return home, rebuild their cities, rebuild their temple, and worship their God as they chose. Some of the people returned, and between 520 and 515 BC the temple was rebuilt. Under the leadership of Nehemiah in 444 and 432 BC, Jerusalem was rebuilt and repopulated. During this time, however, the people of Judah were politically part of the Persian Empire, and later the Greek Empire, which arose after the conquest of the area by Alexander the Great. The Jewish people remained part of those political structures until 141 BC when Judah became an independent political state. This situation continued for almost 100 years until the Romans took over the area. Thus both of the so-called "unfulfilled prophecies" were in fact fulfilled. The prophetic oracles were not referring to the nineteenth, twentieth, or twenty-first centuries AD.

Darby and his followers believed strongly, however, that God had to deal with the world through the nation Israel, and they continued to decipher how that could happen since the establishment of the church. They believed that the church was only a temporary afterthought that began at Pentecost (or with Paul's ministry or when Paul went to Rome). It became necessary because the Jewish nation had rejected Jesus as their Messiah. In order for God to renew dealing with the earth through Israel, something had to occur that would remove the church from the world and that would inaugurate the "final" history of the world.

## The Rapture and the Great Tribulation

The answer to the problem of the removal of the church was found in the concept of the "rapture." The church, it was believed, would be caught out of the world, i.e., raptured, removed from earth to heaven, so that God could once again act in history through the nation Israel. Since Darby believed the church was corrupt and "in ruins," it was not a great loss for the world to lose the church. After all, only a few people in the church were true believers. The idea of a rapture came from 1 Thessalonians 4:17: "Then we who are alive, who are left, shall be caught up together with them in the clouds to meet the Lord in the air," In this passage it seems clear that whatever Paul intended by this idea he meant it to be understood as occurring *at the time* of the Parousia, i.e., the time of Jesus' return. Darby moved the rapture, however, to accommodate the necessity for the removal of the church in his schema.

Since this rapture of the church was to occur before Christ's coming, some of Darby's followers devised the idea of a two-stage return of Jesus, something biblical passages do not support. One can see that the biblical passages have been forced to fit the preconceived notion. Darby believed that the end was near, and the emphasis upon the rapture came to be known as the "at-any-moment coming of Jesus." Some of his followers held that the rapture would be a secret event, that is, it would happen but no one left would actually be aware of it. Some Darbyists still hold to this idea, but most have disregarded it.

As already mentioned, the majority of people in the church through the centuries had basically held to a *post*millennial view of the return of Jesus. Jesus was to return after a 1,000-year rule of the saints on earth. According to Darby's ideas, however, such a view could not possibly be correct. Jesus still had to sit on David's throne on the earth and rule over the nation Israel. In order for this to occur, Jesus would have to return *before* the millennium; thus Darby and his followers have been consistently premillennial in their interpretation regarding the return of Jesus.

Another motif was developed and refined by Darby and his followers. This idea is known as "the Great Tribulation." One of the key ideas in apocalyptic thinking was that before a new age dawned there would be a period of persecution and suffering for the people of God. Many of the New Testament passages that refer to Jesus' return and the establishment of the new age naturally follow the apocalyptic formula and include a period of persecution immediately preceding those events. (Whether these ideas were intended to be understood literally or symbolically need not detain us at this point.) Darby and his followers have made the "seventy weeks of years" of Daniel 9 a key point of understanding with regard to this "tribulation."

According to them, the seventy weeks of years began sometime after the return of the Jewish people from Babylonia to Palestine. According to their interpretation, 490 years after this prediction in Daniel 9:24-27, the new messianic kingdom was supposed to begin. The popular term to describe these 490 years seems to be "God's prophetic stopwatch." By beginning to count at various historical times and by using 360 days as the length of a year (depending on the group within the system), the

Darbyists have come up with the idea that it was 438 years from the time mentioned in Daniel until Jesus was publicly proclaimed Messiah. Since the Jewish people rejected Jesus, however, "God's prophetic stopwatch" was put on hold. It will not restart until the Great Tribulation, which will last for seven years (i.e., the last "week of years" of the Daniel passage). The fact that the book of Daniel knows nothing of a stopping of the clock and that the passage refers to the kingdom ultimately set up in 141 BC does not appear to bother these interpreters.

Another problem to be solved was the question of when the rapture would occur—before, during, or after the tribulation. That question is still hotly debated among those who hold to this system. If the rapture takes place during or after the tribulation, the church (or those true believers who are to be taken) will have to participate in the suffering. If the rapture takes place before the tribulation, naturally the favored ones will escape any pain or suffering associated with that evil time. While the debate still continues, the most popular of these ideas is the pre-tribulation rapture.

This entire system of interpretation has come to be known as dispensationalism because of its insistence that God deals with the human race differently in different ages, i.e., *requires* different actions and activity from humanity in different ages or dispensations of human history. The Darbyists claim that the Bible itself speaks of different ages in human history, which it does, but the question arises as to whether these ages were predetermined by God and are therefore part of "God's great plan" or whether the biblical writers spoke of ages of human history simply because history does run through eras or periods of time. The emphasis in the dispensational system on these ages is quite different from what the biblical texts seem to imply.

One of the key passages that led to the idea of predetermined ages came from 2 Timothy 2:15, the last part of which reads, "rightly dividing the word of truth" (KJV). This is a misleading translation, if not wrong, and the *Revised Standard Version* does not improve on it much. If one took the plain meaning of the text (in the translations), it would appear that the author is urging a correct and proper interpretation of "the word of truth." This is not how Darby and his followers have interpreted the text, however. Their idea is that the entire Bible is a prewritten history of the world and of God's dealing with it, and the trick is to decipher the "word" so as to learn how and when and where the end of all the ages will occur. This can be done by deciphering when all the other ages began and ended. In the dispensational system, however, there is no unanimity of agreement as to the number of these ages (or *dispensations*) or when and how many of them were to begin and end. (If the modern reader is willing to wade through some of the more precise arguments and differing ideas, several well-written books offer summaries of the various dispensational systems. These are listed in the bibliography at the conclusion to this book.)

## The Spread of Dispensationalism in America

One may rightly wonder how these ideas, begun by J. N. Darby in Ireland and England, came to be so well known and widely disseminated in the United States. The story is simple in some ways and complex in others, but a clear thread runs through the development of Darby's theology system.

First, Darby was not only a zealot for his theological ideas but an indefatigable worker. In spite of his injured leg, he traveled extensively in Europe and even went to New Zealand. He also made seven visits to the North American continent between 1862 and 1877, partly because some of the people associated with the Brethren movement had come to the United States.

Darby came to America during the bleak years of the Civil War and the following period of Reconstruction. The time was ripe for a message of imminent judgment by God. The fervor of

Darby's presentation and the impact of his considerable intellect attracted many ministers in significant pulpits. Darby wanted the true believers in American churches to form a new group to prepare themselves for the return of Jesus. Much to his surprise and disappointment, the people remained in their denominations, but many of them agreed with Darby's system of interpretation.

Numerous people were helpful in the early stages of the United States movement. Naturally, there was a need for publishing and distributing books and pamphlets that explained the new system. An editor named James Inglis helped explain and distribute Darby's ideas through a journal, *Waymarks in the Wilderness*. Further, a publishing firm founded by two brothers who were part of the Brethren movement, Paul and Timothy Loizeaux, distributed a large amount of dispensational literature.

Another influential person was a Presbyterian minister in St. Louis, James H. Brookes. Brookes was fascinated with Darby and his teaching and became a leading exponent of the system in the U.S. Others were also caught up in the excitement of these fresh ideas. Brookes helped found a series of Bible conferences that met in the summer; they were eventually known as the Niagara Bible Conferences and held from 1875 to 1897. The conferences became a focal point for the leading exponents of Darby's system to come together and share ideas and research about this teaching.

At first the conferences were a rousing success, attracting and exciting many people by offering hope that the Lord might even return before the conference concluded, perhaps even before the meeting ended! It was heady wine, but after a number of years the claims of Jesus' "return at any moment" began to wear thin. Further, some people began to question how one could justify taking bits of passages from various parts of the Bible, disregarding their original setting and meaning, and weaving them into such a system. The stock answer came from Darby himself, who argued that true faith is guided by God's power, not by man's wisdom.

Toward the latter years of the Niagara Bible Conferences, a young attorney became enamored with the system and began to study with Brookes. He learned well and was invited to lecture at Niagara. He was so enthusiastic about the teaching and so zealous for spreading the "truth" that he developed an idea that would, in a sense, revolutionize Bible study. His idea was to publish a Bible with study notes so that laypeople could understand and learn the Darbyist system. He took this idea to the leaders of the Niagra Bible Conferences, hoping to enlist their support. They refused. Not long afterward, the Niagara Bible Conferences folded.

At this point, another figure emerged on the scene—a German immigrant named Arno C. Gaebelein. This man worked among the Jewish community in New York, and some members of the Plymouth Brethren influenced him. Gaebelein met the attorney, and the two began to work closely together. In fact, when the Niagara Bible Conferences folded, the two continued to hold similar conferences in New Jersey. Gaebelein's friend told him about his dream for a Bible that would contain notes to assist readers in understanding Darby's marvelous new system. It so happened that Gaebelein had wealthy friends whom he convinced to support the project. The attorney became a theologian, went to work, and in 1909 published the first edition of the *Scofield Reference Bible*. The attorney's name was Cyrus I. Scofield!

The *Scofield Reference Bible* has had a tremendous influence on the American religious scene. In fact, many people still refer to the Bible as "the Scofield Bible," and this is said with awe and even reverence. What we must remember is that the "Scofield Bible" is the text of the King James Version with Scofield's notes. And we must not forget that the notes are basically the system, interpretations, and ideas that originated with John Nelson

Darby and the Brethren movement. Several revisions of the *Scofield Reference Bible* have altered some of the teachings, but overall the original system remains intact. If we wish to rely on the "Scofield Bible," we must remember where the ideas originated and what presuppositions lie behind the system of interpretation.

Soon after the appearance of the *Scofield Reference Bible*, Scofield and others believed it was time to establish schools in which the dispensational system could be taught. In 1919, Scofield founded an institution called the Philadelphia School of the Bible. One of the first faculty members was Lewis Sperry Chafer. Chafer had met Scofield earlier and had become a devoted follower. As Scofield aged and became less effective (he died in 1921), Chafer took on the mantle of his teacher. He became convinced that a school of higher education should be founded for the purpose of refining and propagating the Darbyist teachings. Thus, in 1924, the Evangelical Theological College was founded; in 1936, it was renamed Dallas Theological Seminary. Chafer became president and wrote a lengthy *Systematic Theology*, setting forth his mature reflections and ideas on the dispensational system.

Today the most well known of the popular teachers of the Darbyist system are Hal Lindsey (*The Late, Great Planet Earth*) and Tim LaHaye (*Left Behind*). Through numerous books and films, both Lindsey and LaHaye have captured the imagination of millions with their teaching. It is, however, the basic teaching enunciated by John Nelson Darby, and it has been around for nearly 175 years.

## The Continuing Success of Darbyist Dispensationalim

One cannot help wondering about the continuing fascination many people have for this type of interpretation. Why is it that after the prediction of the "end" every few years for more than 175 years has never been fulfilled, people would still want to be a part of such a system of interpretation? There are probably numerous answers to this question. First, many are simply over-whelmed with the confidence and seeming brilliance of the Darbyist interpretation. Many passages from the Bible are quoted, and the system of interpretation *appears* to be profound.

Further, these people hold an extremely high view of the Scriptures. They believe it is God's inspired word, the revelation of God to the human race. This is especially important for Protestant Christians, who have always given pride of place to the Bible. Many, if not most, Protestant clergypeople are asked at ordination if they believe the Bible to be God's inspired word, the "only infallible rule of faith and practice." One should note carefully the wording of what is asked, however. There is noth-ing said or implied about infallible science, geography, history, politics, sociology, or the like. The Scripture contains God's rev-elation, which is the only infallible rule of faith and practice, i.e., it is infallible at the point of its religious ideas and understand-ings. The Bible does not give us a history of the world and a literal description of the end of history!

Closely connected with the Darbyists' high view of Scripture is their sincerity. They truly believe what they say they believe. This is the reason for their zeal and industry in espousing their views and seeking to share those views with others. Sincerity, unfortunately, is no guarantee of being right. History is strewn with the bones of many people, religious and otherwise, who were thoroughly convinced of the rightness and correctness of their cause. The fact that the dispensationalists are sincere does not lend support to their interpretation.

This system of interpretation also appeals to humankind's urge to "know" something others either cannot know or cannot understand. Such an attitude is known as "gnostic," from the Greek word *gnosis*, which means knowledge. Some people think they can be saved by knowledge, or since they are saved they think they know and understand matters that remain hidden to others. There is a certain security in such an idea, and this security appeals to many who are attracted to this type of interpretation. Not only do they *know* things others do not know, but they are also going to be protected in the last days by that knowledge or by the system that gives them the knowledge. When engaging people of this persuasion in debate, one notices that many of them react with great emotion because they are not actually discussing a matter of interpretation. To these individuals, any challenge to their interpretation is a threat to their entire faith-security system.

Those who hold to this system of interpretation argue that it should not be rejected merely because it has been around only 175 years. They are correct in this assertion. These advocates also argue that the system and its interpretations should be measured by Scripture itself. Again, they are correct. However, they argue that Scripture is a collection of God's revelation that describes the history of the world and especially predicts the events and personalities that are to be connected with the final days. It is at this point that they go astray. The only presupposition that should be made in approaching the biblical books is to examine the text as honestly and openly as possible to determine as best as we can what the inspired writer originally said and meant. And further, how did the original hearers/readers understand the book? Only when the original meaning is ascertained can we begin to build systems of theology. If we come to the text already knowing what it is going to say, all we find is what we wish to find. This, in effect, is saying that our thoughts are the inspired words of God, not the original biblical books, and that our understandings of what Scripture can and cannot say and mean must be superimposed on the original meaning. It is, in short, the canonization of our thoughts and ideas, and thus the biblical texts are not allowed to speak as originally intended.

To understand the biblical message properly, therefore, the interpreter must be willing to learn about the history, the culture, the settings, and the literary forms and styles of the original author and his intended audience. Further, the "proof-text" method used widely by the Darbyists must be set aside because sentences and phrases taken out of context may be grossly misunderstood and misinterpreted. To take bits of various Scripture texts out of their contexts and weave them together into a scenario that *none* of the biblical writers knew anything about is to do violence to the sacred revelation of God. Such an approach makes human schemes the revelation of God.

Now we will examine the three major areas of the Darbyist system: the rapture (with a look at the Church-Israel idea), the antichrist, and the millennium. What does the Bible say about these three areas? Many will find that some of these ideas are well known today, but not exactly as the "pure" Darbyists have defined the specifics of the system. The grid is basically the same, but a few of the details are different. There is a specific reason for this.

At the end of the nineteenth century and the beginning of the twentieth century, there arose, as most are aware, a conflict between science and religion. Some devoutly religious people believed that the faith and Scripture were under attack. The "enemies" were perceived as trying to destroy religion in general and the Christian faith in particular. Some of them probably were, but the perception of a threat to the faith led a group of people to band together and devise a set of core beliefs that could not be compromised. This movement produced a series of books in the 1920s known as the "Fundamentals of the Christian Faith," promoting basic teachings the group believed were absolutely true and non-negotiable.

The basic theology of this group's thinking was what is known as the TULIP theology. TULIP is an acronym for the five basic theological assumptions these people felt were taught in the Scriptures—total depravity; unconditional election; limited atonement; irresistible grace; and the perseverance of the saints. One can readily see that this system was based on a "super" Calvinistic interpretation of theology. I do not intend to enter into an analysis of this system, but suffice it to say that only one of the elements can claim a solid biblical base—total depravity.

When the time came to complete the theological system, now identified by the term "fundamentalism," with eschatological teachings from the Bible, the Darbyist grid was basically accepted but altered in a few places (e.g., the constituency of the millennial kingdom). At that time, the Darbyist eschatological system had become so widespread that it was nearly the only system known. Therefore, it was incorporated into the theological system of the "fundamentalists." This is the basic background for the proponents of the *Left Behind* phenomenon.

Again, it is not our primary concern to debate every theological detail of the Darbyist system or the fundamentalist system. Our concern is primarily centered on their eschatological teachings, which are nearly the same as far as their grid is presented. They do, however, differ over how the grid is filled in. One must also keep in mind that within the larger groups, there are always smaller groups that deviate a bit from the specifics of their compatriots, but the overall teaching remains the same at the point of the eschatological grid.

This is the grid: the rapture will trigger the "end-times" scenario; there will be a seven-year period of the "Great Tribulation," usually divided into two segments of three and a half years each; then there is usually depicted the great battle of Armageddon, which occurs in some connection with the premillennial return of Jesus; after his return, Jesus establishes the earthly reign of 1,000 years. (Some think, however, that the battle of Armegeddon will occur after the millennial kingdom.) Last is the final judgment.

As those who are familiar with the *Left Behind* books will recognize, this is the basic structure contained and presented in those stories. Even though the people, times, and specifics depicted in those books are supposed to be fictional, the clear intent of the series is to present what occurs to these fictional characters as specifically "predicted" biblical teaching.

## Questions for Study and Discussion

1. In the church today, are there ideas or actions related to "end times" teachings that cause divisiveness? If so, what are they? How should we approach them?

2. Read 2 Timothy 2:14ff. What does this text teach about dividing history into ages? What does it say or not say about the way God deals with the world or when the Parousia might come?

3. In what ways can we find the influence of the Darby dispensationalists in our churches today?

# CHAPTER 3

# The Rapture

One of the key components of the dispensational, eschatological system, and notably the popular *Left Behind* series of books and films, is the idea of the rapture, the "snatching up" of the true believers in the church before the "evil times" begin. The Darbyists argue among themselves about the timing of this major event, but all affirm its literal reality. Some of these theologians believe the rapture will occur before the Great Tribulation, some during it, and others afterward. These are known, respectively, as pre-tribulationists, mid-tribulationists, and post-tribulationists. All are, of course, premillenial, believing that Jesus will return *before* his 1,000-year earthly reign over the nation Israel. (How the church or the Christian saints will participate in this scenario is also hotly debated.)

Before examining the idea of the rapture itself, one must examine the fundamental idea of the dispensational system that Israel and the church are always separate and that God deals with this world through the literal historical nation of Israel.

Some of the arguments for this rigid separation stem from alleged "unfulfilled prophecies" dealing with the nation of Judah in Old Testament literature, and some of these ideas have already been discussed. Perhaps the most important passages related to this concept in the Darbyist system are those that relate to the covenants and promises made to Abraham and to David. God promises that Abraham will inherit the land forever and that David will have a house (i.e., dynasty) forever (cf. Gen 17:1-8; 2 Sam 7:4-17). It is unfortunate that English translators continue to render the Hebrew of these passages "forever." The Hebrew mind-set did not have a concept of "forever" in the Greek mode; when the Hebrews used the term translated "forever" (literally, it means "to the age"), it usually carried the connotation of either a long undefined period of time or a unit of time with a specific or definite conclusion. For example, in Job 7:16a Job says, "I loathe my life; I would not live for ever." What is meant here is that Job does not want to live out his allotted time; his suffering is so great that as precious as life is, he wishes to forfeit his remaining days to escape the pain of his existence. There is no meaning of our idea of forever in this passage.

Thus one can already begin to understand that the promises made to Abraham and to David were not forever in a modern understanding of that term. Further, there is the idea (prevalent among numerous groups today) that the promises and covenants made to Abraham and to David were unconditional, that God gave them with no strings attached. The truth is that in reading the biblical books it becomes clear that there is no such thing as an unconditional promise by God that does not require and depend upon human response. One certainty in the Scriptures is that God cannot be bound by anything or anyone. The basic problem with the human race is its insistence that God do its bidding rather than vice versa. God, in acts of graciousness, offers all sorts of good things to humankind but always with two prerequisites: (1) that the gifts be accepted on

God's terms and (2) that the gifts be used for the accomplish-
ment of God's purposes in the world. God's promises are always
contingent upon the proper response by human beings. In
Romans 9–11, Paul makes this point clear in his discussion of
the rejection of Israel as being God's uniquely elected people. In
each of these chapters, Paul writes that inappropriate human
response frees God from any "absolute" adherence to promises
made (cf. Rom 9:25-32; 10:1-3, 21; 11:17-24). God's purposes
will ultimately be brought to fruition—that is clear—but the
people through whom those purposes are to be accomplished are
always open to God's call, and a proper response is required
from them.

The Darbyists, however, insist that their understandings of
God's promises made to the nation Israel must be fulfilled. God
has no real choice in the matter according to this line of reasoning. Fundamental to the idea is the absolute distinction between
Israel and the church. One of the leading proponents of dispensational theology has said, "The essence of dispensationalism,
then, is the distinction between Israel and the Church. . . . The
term *Israel* continues to be used [i.e., in the New Testament
writings] for the natural (not spiritual) descendants of Abraham
after the Church was instituted, and it is not equated with the
Church."[1]

This line of argument is supported by adherents of the dispensational system by appeals to various verses (or parts of
verses) in the New Testament, usually requiring some twisting of
the texts to arrive at the needed explanation. One such verse is
Galatians 6:16. The verse reads, "Peace and mercy be upon all
who walk by this rule, upon the Israel of God." In context, it is
clear that Paul refers to those who have become a part of the
Christian community whether they were from Jewish or Gentile
backgrounds. Distinctions in such things as circumcision, for
example, have no place in determining who belongs to the new
people of God. Such an understanding means the new Christian

community is called the "Israel of God," something the Darbyists cannot allow. Therefore, the interpretation many of them give for this passage is based upon a misinterpretation of the Greek text.

In the Greek text, the word *kai* is found before the phrase "upon the Israel of God." The normal meaning of that word in this context is "even." The Darbyists, however, interpret the word as "and." From that understanding, they argue that there is a clear-cut distinction between the church and Israel. Others argue that the Israel referred to here consists only of Jewish Christians in the Galatian churches. Paul understands Israel to include all those, Jews and Gentiles, who now make up the new people of God, the Christian church.

In fact, the term "Israel" is used in numerous ways in the Bible. It does not always designate the nation Israel. As today, words take meanings from contexts and thus may have several different usages and nuances. The word "Israel" in the Bible refers to the old patriarch (Jacob), the people of God, the land where the people of God lived, the northern nation after the division of David's United Kingdom in 921 BC, southern Judah as God's people after the destruction of northern Israel in 722–721 BC, the restored people of God after the exile (538 BC), and the people of God in the New Testament period. Even though there is no *explicit* statement in the New Testament writings in which the church is called "Israel," in numerous instances there can be no doubt that the followers of Jesus are intended to be understood as the Israel of God. This new Israel of God includes both Jews and Gentiles, as God intended from the original call to Abraham in Genesis 12.

The Darbyists do not acknowledge, however, that the biblical writers use numerous terms in addition to "Israel" to designate the people of God. For example, the terms "people" and "people of God" are used to designate the elect in the Old Testament writings. In the New Testament, there are several references to the

Christian church as the (new) people of God (Rom 9:25; 2 Cor 6:16; Titus 2:14; 1 Pet 2:9-10; Rev 18:4; 21:3). Further, the people of God are frequently called God's "chosen" or "elect" in the Old Testament Scriptures. Likewise, in the New Testament documents the Christian church is designated as God's "chosen" (1 Pet 2:9-10) and the "elect" (Rom 8:33; Col 3:12; Titus 1:1; 2 John 1, 13). Another parallel concerns the use of the term "holy" for God's people. In both the Hebrew and Greek languages, the words for holy have the connotation of someone or something that is "different from" or "other than." God is considered holy because God is different from and other than all created things. God's people are also supposed to be holy, that is, they are to be different from the other peoples of the world by virtue of their calling to do God's special work and by living lives different from the ordinary life in this world. In the Old Testament this idea is found in numerous places, but especially in the Holiness Code of Leviticus where one reads, "Say to all the congregation of the people of Israel, You shall be holy; for I the LORD your God am holy" (Lev 19:2).

In almost every book in the New Testament, except the Gospels, the church is designated by the term "saints." The word for saint in the New Testament writings is *hagios*, which means "holy" or "other than." The church as the people of God are expected to be different from the people of the world by virtue of their calling to do God's special work and by living lives that have a different quality than ordinary human existence. Thus the people of the Christian church are called "saints." There is certainly no doubt in their minds that God is now working through the church to accomplish the goals and purposes originally intended to be accomplished through the people Israel. That this is not a temporary situation or a parenthesis can be clearly seen in Ephesians where the author states that the church is the instrument of God in the world for all the "coming ages" (Eph 2:7).

Many other passages could be cited, but these should be sufficient to demonstrate that the Darbyist idea of the two peoples of God held totally distinct and separate is an *a priori* interpretation forced on the text, not derived from it.

The passage Galatians 6:15-16 has already been discussed, but another one deserves attention—Romans 9:6. In Romans 9–11, Paul struggles mightily with the question of the rejection of the Jewish people and nation as being God's elect people. He argues that God's promises are indeed always valid and God's purposes remain the same. Because of the disbelief and failure of the Jewish people with regard to fulfilling God's elective purpose, God had now chosen a new people to continue the purposes of God in the world.

The reasons for this change are, to Paul, twofold: (1) the mystery of God's mind that is able to see far beyond human intelligence and (2) the failure of the Jewish people to fulfill the purpose God had elected them to do. Many of the Darbyists claim that such an understanding of this text and other New Testament teaching is a form of anti-Semitism. How can people be accused of anti-Semitism when attempting to describe as accurately as possible the meaning of the text? Paul certainly cannot be accused of being anti-Semitic; he wanted his people to be a part of God's plan so much that he was willing to be damned if they could be brought back in (cf. Rom 9:3)! One may wish to differ with the ideas of Paul and the other New Testament writers with regard to their interpretation that the church is indeed the new people of God, replacing the Jewish community as God's chief instrument in the world to proclaim the good news of his revelation and will. However, to make the New Testament writers say something they did not say or intend is to do violence to the sacred text itself. The idea, then, that there is an absolute distinction between Israel and the church, that God deals with the world (i.e., the physical world) through the Jewish nation Israel, that somehow God's "prophetic clock was put on hold" when Israel rejected Jesus as God's messiah are ideas that are *not* in the biblical text. They are imported as part of an a priori understanding or set of understandings that has nothing to do with the obvious meaning of the biblical texts. The idea that Israel is still considered to be *the* intermediary for God's dealing with the world is *not* the teaching of the New Testament. One may wish to believe that Israel is God's chosen even today, but no claim should or can be made that this idea is taught in the New Testament.

As already indicated, the Darbyist system relied heavily on the rapture to remove the Christian church from the scene so that God could resume dealing with the world through the nation Israel, so that "God's prophetic time clock could begin to tick again." Since there is no reason to remove the church from the scene, does this invalidate the concept of rapture? The answer to that question must be negative, but what the rapture is and what the New Testament writings say about it must be judged on the basis of a thorough examination of the texts themselves.

Because of the dispensational emphasis on rapture, there was (and is) a strong tendency on the part of these interpreters to find as many passages as possible that can be understood to refer to this momentous event. Many passages are cited as sources in which the doctrine is taught. For example, the teachings of Jesus presented most commonly in the "wisdom" style (i.e., parable, short pithy sayings, hyperbole) were found to be a good source by the Darbyists, especially when many in the system advocated what some called a "secret rapture." When Jesus gave an account of the end of the age, he was emphasizing the suddenness and swiftness of what was going to happen. In so doing he said, "Then two men will be in the field; one is taken and one is left. Two women will be grinding at the mill; one is taken and one is left" (Matt 24:40-41; cf. the parallel passage in Luke 17:34-35). It is clear that these sayings were figures of speech to emphasize the unexpected and swift nature of what was to occur. If one is already predisposed toward a rapture that takes some people away and leaves others here on earth, it is an easy step for one to use such a passage for support. But the passage(s) cannot and does not bear the weight of that interpretation.

If passages such as these are not references to rapture, where can such passages be found? The simple truth is that there is only *one* passage in the entire New Testament that can be understood as teaching about the rapture. This passage is found in one of Paul's earliest letters, perhaps the earliest of all New Testament books, 1 Thessalonians; the specific passage under consideration is 4:13-18.

In a study of Paul's letters, the interpreter must remember that Paul's writings are all "occasional" in nature. This means the letters were written about specific situations in answer to questions raised by the congregations or to give instructions with regard to problems in the church. In order to understand Paul's teaching, therefore, one must learn as much as possible about the background out of which he speaks and the problems he attempts to solve.

The early church, from which Paul received his basic instruction in the faith after his call, believed strongly in the *early* return of Jesus. They thought this return would take place shortly, surely within their lifetime. (Again, the term used to denote this event is *Parousia.*) Other words were also used (appearing, revelation), but they seem to have been intended as synonyms (something the dispensationalists also debate). The description given of this event was couched in apocalyptic ideology and symbolism. Apocalyptic was a theological thought pattern that arose during the late postexilic period (c. 300–200 BC) and continued until the end of the first century AD. This ideology developed a literary genre characterized by strange symbols and wild images. One of the most characteristic motifs of apocalyptic thought was that before the new age arrived, there would be a period of intense persecution directed against the people of God. After the persecution had run its course, God or God's agent would intervene, remove the persecutor (the persecution was usually concretized in a single individual attempting to eliminate God's people), and establish a new age. The early church naturally utilized this symbolism and terminology to describe the consummation of the kingdom Jesus had come to found. The idea was that after the persecution Jesus would return shortly to consummate the kingdom.

Paul founded the church in Thessalonica on his second journey circa AD 49. He preached to the people the basics of the faith as he understood them at the time, obviously including the nearness of the Parousia. Paul left the area because of animosity against him (Acts 17:1-10). He quickly went to Beroea and Athens, finally settling down for a while in Corinth (early AD 50). Having been "run off" from Thessalonica so quickly, Paul probably did not have time to explicate some of the teachings to the people there. Since the Parousia did not come immediately and since (naturally) people do have a tendency to die as life goes on, the new Christians in Thessalonica had two basic questions: What had happened to their loved ones who had died? And would they miss out on the joys of the final consummation of God's kingdom in the Parousia? Paul responds to these two questions in his discussion in 1 Thessalonians 4:13-18 (cf. 5:1-11):

> [13]But we would not have you ignorant, brethren, concerning those who are asleep, that you may not grieve as others do who have no hope. [14]For since we believe that Jesus died and rose again, even so, through Jesus, God will bring with him those who have fallen asleep. [15]For this we declare to you by the word of the Lord, that we who are alive, who are left until the coming of the Lord, shall not precede those who have fallen asleep. [16]For the Lord himself will

descend from heaven with a cry of command, with
the archangel's call, and with the sound of the trum-
pet of God. And the dead in Christ will rise first;
[17]then we who are alive, who are left, shall be caught
up together with them in the clouds to meet the Lord
in the air; and so we shall always be with the Lord.
[18]Therefore comfort one another with these words.

The first impression the reader senses in reading this passage
is Paul's sensitive response to those experiencing pain over the
loss of loved ones. He tells the Thessalonian Christians that they
should not grieve as those "who have no hope." One notes that
Paul does not say grieving is wrong or unchristian (some, unfortunately, have used or misread this passage in that way), and he
reminds the people that their hope lies in the resurrection of
Jesus. Since Jesus has conquered death, so those who are united
to God share in this great victory. Therefore, those who have
already died, rather than being in a secondary position with
regard to the final victory of God, are in a primary position. The
reason for this is that they are already with the Lord. They are in
a real sense already experiencing the joys of the final consummation. This seems to be what Paul means by the expression "The
dead in Christ will rise first."

The second question is, therefore, partially answered by the
response to the first. Paul, however, goes on to give a description
of the Parousia in which he says, "Then we who are alive, who
are left, shall be caught up together with them in the clouds to
meet the Lord in the air." This passage specifically serves as the
basis for the concept of rapture, and there are two ways in which
it can be legitimately interpreted.

The first is to understand Paul's statement here as absolutely
literal. When the Parousia occurs, it will be a physical event,
obvious to the naked human eye, and at that time the Christian
believers who are alive on the earth will be literally lifted up into

the air to meet the returning Jesus. One notes with some interest that there is no evidence whatsoever that this event occurs before the return of Jesus as the Darbyists claim. Whatever happens occurs simultaneously with the return.

The second possible interpretation of this passage is symbolic. Those who take the verses in this way argue that Paul is trying to describe something that is in a human sense indescribable and does so by the use of apocalyptic symbols. This means Paul probably intended the entire scenario to be taken symbolically. In such an approach, the term "in the air" would simply have the connotation of being with God and Christ "in heaven," which in spatial terms would be "up." When the "last things" occur, the people of God will be together in their relationship with God and Christ.

One of the most telling arguments for this passage to be understood symbolically is that two other passages in the Pauline literature seem to describe the same event. However, interpreting those two passages literally (along with this one in 1 Thessalonians) gives three *different* literal interpretations of the same event. This means Paul is at odds with himself; and two of the passages, if all are to be understood as literally true, must be thrown out as contradictory with the one chosen!

The first and most important of these other passages is found in 1 Corinthians 15:42-57, especially verses 50-53. In this passage, Paul responds to three questions put to him by the people in Corinth with regard to the resurrection. First, the Corinthians wanted to know if Jesus *really* rose from the dead. Second, they wanted to know if Christians would also participate in a resurrection; since the resurrection of Christ was unique, would they and their loved ones already gone really participate in the triumph of life known as resurrection? Finally, the question was raised, what kind of body does one get in the resurrected state?

Paul speaks to each of these concerns, and the interpreter can follow his arguments by reading through the chapter. Our concern here is with the latter point, 15:50-53. Here Paul still believes in an early return of Jesus: "We shall not all sleep [i.e., die], but we shall all be changed." The account of what is to happen appears to be a description of the same event depicted in 1 Thessalonians 4:13-18. In 1 Corinthians, however, there is no mention of a "transporting" of people into the air. Paul describes here a "transmutation," i.e., a changing of the basic makeup of believers so that they can now participate in a spiritual existence.

The question then arises as to how Paul could describe what appears to be essentially the same event but in such different terminology. If one recalls that Paul is attempting to explain in human terminology things no human fully understands, one can ascertain why the accounts are different. They are symbolic depictions of a fundamental belief that believers are to be with God always, that physical death does not break the believer's relationship with God, and that when the final consummation of God's work in Christ does occur, all of God's people will be given "bodies" suitable for life in a spiritual dimension.

It is clear that Paul believes something special and unique is going to occur at the time of the Parousia. Exactly what that is cannot be described, but Paul made several attempts to do so in response to questions asked by these two church groups. Each answer is different because each is done in response to specific questions, and each is done in symbolic figures. One notes with great interest that whatever occurs is to take place *at the same time* as the Parousia. There is absolutely no justification in the biblical texts for moving this event in order to remove the true believers from the world so that God can once again deal with the world through the historical Jewish nation.

There is yet another passage that is sometimes used as a supplementary text for the rapture idea—2 Thessalonians 2. If one examines the passage carefully, even the comments in 2

Thessalonians 1, one finds that there is no reference in this letter to a rapture. The passage does have significance for an interpretation of antichrist, which will be discussed in the following chapter.

The truth is that there are no other passages in the entire New Testament that can be linked with the idea of a rapture. There are numerous passages to which those who hold to a doctrine of rapture appeal, however. None of these, understood in the proper context of their own settings, even hint at rapture. Perhaps an examination of one of these passages will suffice to illustrate the point.

The book of Revelation, an apocalyptic work, is one of the key biblical writings with regard to matters pertaining to end times for those preoccupied with such things. Naturally, evidence for a rapture will be found there, whether it exists or not. For example, one such interpretation emphasizes the fact that after chapter 3 in the book of Revelation, the literal word "church" is not found until the last chapter of the book. According to some of the Darbyists, that means the church has been "raptured" out of the world and the rest of Revelation (until the last few chapters) describes the seven years of tribulation.

The passage in 4:5 that mentions the "seven torches of fire" is interpreted as the church raptured into heaven, since in 1:12-20 the figure of the "seven golden lampstands" is interpreted as the church. If one looks at the passage carefully, however, one finds that the "seven torches of fire" are further defined as "the seven spirits of God." This term was used earlier (1:4) to represent the Holy Spirit. Seven lampstands are not the same as seven torches, and when the text plainly describes the seven torches as the seven spirits (i.e., the Holy Spirit), it is presumptuous to interpret the seven torches as representing the "raptured" church.

Whatever the rapture is, it is not a device to get the true believers out of the world before Jesus returns. The New Testament texts simply do not teach such a belief. To argue this line of interpretation is simply another illustration of presuppositions and preunderstandings being read *into* the text. One cannot get that meaning (and the idea of the church and Israel being two separate and totally distinct entities) *out of* the text itself.

## Notes

[1] C.C. Ryrie, *Dispensationalism Today* (Chicago: Moody Press, 1965), 47, 138.

[2] For a fuller, popular exposition of this mode of interpretation see the works of Hal Lindsey

## Questions for Study and Discussion

1. What do you think we should do when confronted by "theological systems" that claim biblical support? Do you think people sometimes interpret Scripture to fit into their systems? How can we identify this mistake and avoid it in our own reading of the Bible?

2. Carefully compare 1 Thessalonians 4:13ff with 1 Corinthians 15:50ff. Do you think both teachings can be literally true? Why or why not?

3. What are your beliefs about the rapture? On what do you base these beliefs?

4. How have contemporary depictions of the rapture outside of the biblical record influenced your beliefs about the rapture?

# CHAPTER 4

# The Antichrist

After the belief that God must remove the church from the scene before the end times can begin (which is made possible by the rapture), the next major component in the Darbyist system is the occurrence of the Great Tribulation, usually ruled by the antichrist. Exactly where the idea of a period of intense persecution originated and how the dispensational system understands that idea must be examined before moving on to the antichrist.

Apocalyptic ideology as it developed in Hebrew culture in the postexilic period came to view history (especially present history) as being divided into two ages. One was a present evil age under the dominion of evil forces from which there was no hope of redemption except through the direct intervention of God. The second or new age was viewed as a glorious time for the people of God because God had removed the evil source(s) of persecution. Once history resumed its normal course, life would go on until the arrival of a new period of persecution. Thus the idea was widespread in apocalyptic thought that before a new age could begin, there would be a period of persecution. Such descriptions are found in several places in the Scriptures (e.g., Mark 13; 2 Thess 2).

The Darbyists have utilized this concept to argue for what they have designated as the seven-year period of tribulation. Their reference is basically Daniel (especially 9:24-27) and the presupposition made that there would be 70 weeks of years, i.e., 490 years from that time in Daniel until the New Messianic Kingdom would be established. It has been noted already that God's prophetic stopwatch was put on hold at 483 years. What is going to happen in these last seven years when the stopwatch begins again? That will be the time of the Great Tribulation. (One notes with interest that the advocates of this system cannot agree on the details here either, some dividing the seven-year period into two segments of three and one-half years each). The New Testament passage commonly used to support this idea comes from the apocalyptic passage in Mark 13 in which Jesus describes the coming destruction of Jerusalem and the temple (see Mark 13:19 and especially the parallel in Matt 24:21; one notes that Luke omits the specific reference to a persecution, though he describes a heavy scene [Luke 21:20-24]). In typical apocalyptic imagery, the events connected with this occasion are dramatized in hyperbole, and the description utilizes the concept of increased persecution before the beginning of a new age. Combining these elements from the various parts of Scripture, the Darbyists have devised the scenario of the Great Tribulation that will occur immediately before the return of Jesus to begin the millennial kingdom here on earth, fulfilling the covenants made with Israel.

It is clear in the New Testament teaching that the idea of a persecution of God's people before the new age begins was widely held. It is also clear that this teaching was presented in apocalyptic imagery. Whether it is legitimate to literalize symbolic apocalyptic imagery and ideas into specific scenes of persecution is open to question. It is also clear that the vast majority of the dispensationalists hold to a pre-tribulational rapture, meaning that the true people of God will be taken away before the persecution begins. This is a comforting thought, but it is not what the texts say. The people of God are always involved in and suffer through the persecution (or "tribulation").

The ideas the Darbyists connect with the concept of this Great Tribulation are dubious in most respects and downright wrong in others. It is, however, within this alleged period of tribulation in the dispensational system that the figure of the antichrist arises. There have been numerous attempts to identify this figure with some contemporary person or institution.

It was characteristic of Hebrew thought and culture to epitomize or concretize entire movements or eras in one person or personality, usually the name of the person thought to have inaugurated the movement. For example, since Moses was the first great lawgiver, all law goes back to Moses. Solomon was the first to champion the wisdom movement in Israel, so all wisdom goes back to Solomon. Thus when persecution came, these people usually spoke as if all the persecution were centered in the one who was considered the leader of the persecution. And if there had been an especially evil person or nation who led that persecution, subsequent periods of persecution were often spoken of as caused by the same evil person or nation. This does not mean people believed such entities could or would literally "rise from the dead," but frequently designations and names from earlier periods of persecution were used to symbolize a new present situation. When such thinking was merged with apocalyptic symbolism and imagery, numerous descriptions of former hated persecutors were depicted as occurring once again.

In the book of Daniel, for example, the persecutor (Antiochus IV Epiphanes, ruler of the Seleucid Empire) is depicted as a "little horn with a big mouth" (Dan 7:8, 20, 25; 8:9-12, 23-25; 11:36-39). In the book of Revelation, the perse-

cutor (the Roman Empire) is pictured as a beast (Rev 13) and as
a harlot seated on a beast (Rev 17). To the people who understood the apocalyptic thought pattern and apocalyptic
symbolism, there was no real mystery about what these images
represented.

The early church fervently believed that Jesus was going to
return within their generation to consummate God's kingdom.
When the early New Testament writers attempted to describe
this event, they usually used apocalyptic images and symbols. An
example of this type of description exists in 2 Thessalonians 2:3-
10. In fact, this is the only passage in the New Testament that
depicts in any detail the events leading up to the Parousia.

> [3]Let no one deceive you in any way; for that day will
> not come, unless the rebellion comes first, and the
> man of lawlessness is revealed, the son of perdition,
> [4]who opposes and exalts himself against every so-
> called god or object of worship, so that he takes his
> seat in the temple of God, proclaiming himself to be
> God. [5]Do you not remember that when I was still
> with you I told you this? [6]And you know what is
> restraining him now so that he may be revealed in his
> time. [7]For the mystery of lawlessness is already at
> work; only he who now restrains it will do so until he
> is out of the way. [8]And then the lawless one will be
> revealed, and the Lord Jesus will slay him with the
> breath of his mouth and destroy him by his appearing
> and his coming. [9]The coming of the lawless one by
> the activity of Satan will be with all power and with
> pretended signs and wonders, [10]and with all wicked
> deception for those who are to perish, because they
> refused to love the truth and so be saved.

This letter obviously was addressed to the people in the
church at Thessalonica. The author attempts to encourage the

church to keep the faith in the face of persecution (2 Thess 1:5-6). Given the circumstances at the time, it would be natural for an author to write in apocalyptic imagery. Further, there were reports that this church had received a letter purporting to be from Paul that claimed the Parousia had already come. These two issues are closely related since the idea in the early church was that the Parousia would be preceded by a period of persecution. As is true today, many were ready to claim that the final days had come upon them. Paul wrote to the people at Thessalonica about the specific situation.

Chapter 2 of 2 Thessalonians was a refutation of the idea circulating that the Parousia had come. Paul argues that this event could not have occurred without certain conditions being met first. In typical apocalyptic imagery, Paul describes a period of persecution in which the faithful must struggle not to become apostate and the appearance of a person who would be the leader of the forces of evil against the people of God. This person is called "the man of lawlessness" (2:3; in some early texts, "the man of sin"). The symbolism here is obviously taken from or is a reflection of the similar situation in Daniel (Dan 8:9-14; 9:24-27; 11:21-45) where the people were experiencing a severe persecution. Some scholars have attempted to make an exact identification of this figure in 2 Thessalonians (such as the Roman emperor Gaius), but such an identification seems futile. Paul does not identify this person specifically, believing that whoever it is will come in the *near* future (near to Paul's time, not ours).

Given the symbolic nature of apocalyptic thinking, it is possible that Paul did not have anyone or anything specific in mind as this "man of lawlessness." It appears that he again speaks generally in traditional symbolic imagery to describe a scene he does not know how to depict with specifics. Paul always realized, as some others have not, that the future belongs to God and will be worked out by God. What Paul is certain about is that God will consummate the kingdom and win the final victory whenever and however God chooses to do it.

It is interesting that the term "antichrist" is never used in this passage even though it is one of the chief components for the description of this person or being for those who speculate about such matters. In fact, the word "antichrist" is used in the New Testament writings in only one place—the Johannine letters. In that setting, the term is clearly defined:

> Children, it is the last hour; and as you have heard that antichrist is coming, so now many antichrists have come. . . . This is the antichrist, he who denies the Father and the Son (1 John 2:18-22).

> By this you know the Spirit of God: every spirit which confesses that Jesus Christ has come in the flesh is of God, and every spirit which does not confess Jesus is not of God. This is the spirit of antichrist, of which you heard that it was coming, and now it is in the world already (1 John 4:2-3).

> For many deceivers have gone out into the world, men who will not acknowledge the coming of Jesus Christ in the flesh; such a one is the deceiver and the antichrist (2 John 7).

Those are the only passages in the entire New Testament in which the term "antichrist" is used. In this setting, the antichrist is defined as anyone who denies the reality of the human Jesus.

In addition, two passages refer to "false Christs" (Mark 13:22 and Matt 24:24), but obviously since there are numerous false messiahs these references cannot be the antichrist. The only conclusion to which one can legitimately come is that the figure of the antichrist is another imported idea read into and not out of the biblical texts.

There are yet one or two passages from the book of Revelation to which the advocates of a specifically predicted antichrist appeal for support of their ideas. They are chapters 13 and 17 of Revelation. Revelation was written to Christians in Asia Minor (present-day Turkey) to bolster their faith in a time of persecution. Late in the first century, the Roman Empire through Emperor Domitian attempted to foster the worship of the state and emperor in that part of the empire. Some people had actually lost their lives (Rev 2:13; 6:9-11), and others were finding it difficult to maintain a normal lifestyle in the community (Rev 13:17). In accordance with the times, the author wrote to these people in typical apocalyptic symbolism.

In apocalyptic literature, one of the chief characteristics was for the author to depict "scenes" in the form of visions. These visionary scenes are usually self-contained and have specific ideas and principles that are carefully proclaimed through the imagery contained in the vision. Further, there is usually a heavenly guide accompanying the seer so as to explain clearly the meaning of the vision. (The idea that the apocalyptic writings were done in some sort of code so that the persecutors could not understand the message does not bear the weight of careful examination.) The symbolism of the figures is usually quite plain, and the symbolism that is not (or could be misunderstood) is clearly explained for the hearer/reader. Also, in almost every apocalyptic work there is a historical survey giving a symbolic description of what had led to the present period of persecution and who was doing the persecuting. For example, there are several in the book of Daniel (see especially chs. 7 and 8).

In the book of Revelation, two passages, chapters 13 and 17, are used to define and identify the one persecuting the Christians. Perhaps chapter 13 is the passage most heavily utilized at this point. To understand why people have viewed this passage as a prediction of some great enemy of God and God's people to come in the future, one must again recall that apocalyptic thought and literature flourished from circa 200 BC–AD 100, and it basically flourished in Jewish (and later Christian) circles. When the Christian movement became primarily a Gentile entity, apocalyptic thought and style became less and less a central part of Christian theology. Further, because the Christians had relied so heavily on apocalyptic ideas, the Jewish community tended to turn its back on apocalyptic writing and admitted only one book into the canon that was decidedly apocalyptic (Daniel, chs. 7–12). All the other apocalyptic books (and they were numerous) were denied acceptance to the Hebrew canon. Most of the apocalyptic writings were then lost, and the key to understanding this type of literature was quickly lost as well.

Because apocalyptic ideology was such a part of the New Testament thought processes (almost all New Testament books are affected by apocalyptic ideology in some way), it was not a simple matter to dissociate the Christian community from this type of thinking. How did one understand this literature, however? Many were puzzled and simply left those parts of the New Testament alone, especially the interpretation of the book of Revelation. Then as now, however, some were eager to sensationalize these teachings and figures by claiming esoteric knowledge about the end of the world and the return of Jesus. Because of this, the marvelous book of Revelation almost was not accepted into the canon of New Testament. As all know, the book was accepted, but few people knew how to interpret it properly. Therefore, in the history of the early and medieval church there is probably less emphasis on its interpretation than on any of the longer New Testament writings. There was much speculation about this strange book, and some interpretation was done, but no one seemed to feel comfortable with it. Most people focused on the millennium primarily and secondarily on the figure of the beast in chapter 13.

Since the return of Jesus had not taken place and since the book of Revelation was not understood properly (owing to its apocalyptic nature), many in the church felt that Revelation must be the description of what would happen at the end. The beast, therefore, became a part of the church's thinking as it was identified with the epitome of evil that would precede the return of Jesus. Thus people began to speculate about the identity of the beast, especially those who were convinced that the end was near. Through the years, the beast has been identified with the Muslim Empire (at the time of the Crusades) with Saladin as the wounded head come back to life. At the time of the Protestant Reformation, the Roman Catholic Church and the pope were the nominees, and the Protestant movement and its leaders were also suggested by the other side! During the latter part of the eighteenth and the beginning of the nineteenth centuries, the French Republic and Napoleon held this honor. In the last century, the Germans under Kaiser Wilhelm and later the Third Reich and Adolf Hitler were the likely suspects. During the Second World War, Japan and Italy with General Hideki Tojo, the Emperor Hirohito, and Benito Mussolini were suggested. After that war, Russia and Joseph Stalin, Red China, North Korea, North Vietnam, and Ayatollah Khomeini have been "ciphered out" as the beastly antichrist. (Even Henry Kissinger was believed by some to be this figure!) That some of these people (and nations at certain times) have been embodiments of demonic evil is plainly true, but the text of Revelation certainly does not specifically predict any of these.

Another element factored into the scheme by the more extreme Darbyists arose from the reference in Revelation 13:16-17 to a "mark" those on the side of the beast received. At one period, Social Security numbers were attacked as a fulfillment of that prophecy. Today the Universal Product Code on packages has been widely suggested to be the mark. Another interesting idea is that there is a giant computer in Belgium (affectionately known as "The Beast") from which everyone will receive a number. It is argued that each person's number will occur in

three groups of six numbers each (666). Another of the more
popular interpretations is that the beast is the European
Common Market and from that group will arise a powerful and
evil leader who will turn out to be the antichrist. In fact, it is
argued that this person is alive today! One could continue to
enumerate these speculative identifications *ad infinitum.*

It should be plain to anyone who reads the book of
Revelation with any degree of objectivity that the author is
describing something that was going on *in his own time.* The
book's readers experienced the persecution the author described,
and they understood the meaning of the symbols. To read into
this text modern meanings and personalities as having been
cryptically predicted is to do violence to the sacred text and in
essence tell the text what it can and cannot say and mean. That
is nothing short of canonizing one's own ideas rather than allowing God's revelation to speak through the inspired text. The
most logical approach would be to examine these two texts,
Revelation 13 and 17, to ascertain what they said and meant.

As noted earlier, apocalyptic writing usually takes the form
of a series of visions, each one self-contained. And in apocalyptic
works there are frequently occasions in which two or more
visions may have essentially the same meaning. This appears to
be the case in these two passages. Chapter 13 is part of a larger
unit, chapters 12–14, and chapter 17 is part of a larger unit,
chapters 17–19. Both units describe the persecution the people
experienced and depict the persecutor in symbolic images.
Further, there is the symbolic description of the removal of the
persecutor (14:17-20; chs. 18–19, especially 19:11-21). In order
to understand what is being said, it is necessary to examine carefully each of these chapters.

First, one notes that chapter 13 continues the scene begun in
chapter 12, where the reason for the persecution of God's people
is given. Satan, the epitome of cosmic evil, has failed in his
attempt to destroy God's Messiah and has turned his wrath

upon the people of God (symbolized by the woman). To assist him in this struggle, Satan summons a hideous beast from the sea and gives him power and authority. In apocalyptic writing, beasts represent nations, and heads on beasts represent rulers. The passage here appears to be exactly that. The curious point lies in the description where one of the heads appears to have died and come back to life (see more below).

This beast is given dominion over all the earth and makes war on the saints. It is a simple matter to ask what nation at that time ruled over all the earth and what nation at that time was persecuting Christians in Asia Minor. The answer to both questions is Rome. To assist the first beast in its zeal for power and respect, a second beast appears and is given authority to compel people to worship the first beast. Indeed, a religious cultus was then in place in Asia Minor with its headquarters in Pergamum (see Rev 2:13) that was doing just that. The description of the deceits practiced in the cultus (13:11-15) is similar to those practiced in other pagan temples, and the deceits are well documented in ancient writings. The important point is that this cultus had the authority to deny people access to the marketplace and other normal areas of life, indicating that it was closely linked to the political sources of power. The reference to having a mark probably refers to the practice of branding slaves or religious zealots to show who owned them. Whether this mark in Revelation was intended to be understood literally or symbolically is irrelevant here.

At this point in the description, the beast is more specifically identified. Note that the beast is *not* called *antichrist*; neither is it depicted as someone or something to come in the future. Whatever it is, it is contemporary with the people addressed by the writer, i.e., the Christians of Asia Minor circa AD 90–95. The author tells the readers/hearers who the beast is by designating its number. To modern thinking, this is cryptic mystery, but to the people of that time there was no real problem in understanding the figure. In those days, many peoples counted by using letters of the alphabet (the Arabic system of numerals was not introduced until the Middle Ages), and specific numerical designations were assigned to each letter of an alphabet. In such a system, a name became more than a name alone; it was also a number. The phrase in the text, "it is a human number," means in Greek that this was a "man's name."

There is a problem with the number in the Greek texts, however. While some ancient Greek manuscripts read 666, others read 616. We must also raise the question about the wounded head on the beast. What does it mean? It appears fairly obvious that a single person must provide the answer to all three of these problems. Mention has already been made of the practice of the Hebrew and early Christian communities to concretize entire movements in the person who began the movement. Since it is almost certain that the beast represents Rome, the heads will then represent Roman emperors. The one singled out is the wounded head that was healed. The beast is represented as the persecutor of the people of God, as Rome was doing in this particular area at this time.

The first Roman emperor to persecute Christians was the infamous Nero. About AD 63–64 Nero wanted to tear down a section of Rome in order to build a pet project. When the Roman senate refused to go along with the plan, Nero had that section of the city torched. The scheme, however, backfired on Nero so that he had to look for a scapegoat. This he found in the relatively new religious movement in town, the Christians. Nero had some of these people crucified, some impaled, some dressed in animal skins and wild dogs released on them, and some dipped in tar, tied in trees, and set afire to become human torches for the parties in his gardens. This persecution occurred around AD 64–66. It was a desperate time for the Christians in Rome. Nero finally committed suicide, but rumors persisted that it was a double whose body had been discovered and that he had fled to Parthia (old Persia) and would sometime return to reclaim the emperorship. Finally, after circa AD 88, it was thought that Nero was actually dead, but then a belief arose that he would rise from the dead. (People have difficulty believing that demonic evil can die, as was evidenced with Adolf Hitler after the Second World War.) Given this historical setting originally, the stage was set for the idea that Nero would be reborn.

Obviously neither the author of Revelation nor the Christians actually believed (as some others did) that Nero would literally rise from the dead. With the persecution of the Christians by Domitian, a Roman emperor, they could, however, believe that Nero had been reborn in Domitian. That identification could and would explain the reference to the wounded head that had healed, but there is still the problem of 666 and 616. Numerous ideas have been proposed with regard to this number problem, but the solution accepted by a vast majority of respectable New Testament scholars is that the numbers represent the two spellings of Nero's name and title in Aramaic.

One may legitimately ask why the name would be spelled in Aramaic. A careful study of Revelation reveals strong Semitic tendencies and figures in the book. This is one consideration. Further, there are tendencies in apocalyptic literature to use figures, symbols, and designations from "foreign" backgrounds. This would explain the spelling of *Neron Caesar* in Aramaic (which yields 666) and the variant spelling *Nero Caesar* (which yields 616). The figure of Nero, the first emperor who persecuted the Christians, explains all three of the problems, i.e., the wounded head, 666, and 616. And it certainly fits into the time and place in which Revelation was written.

Chapter 17 closely resembles chapter 13. Here, however, the figure is that of a Great Harlot sitting on a scarlet beast. It is obvious from the description of the beast that it is intended to be the same as that in chapter 13. The beast, one recalls, represents a nation. The woman in this instance is a parody of the woman in chapter 12 who represented the people of God. This harlot is called Babylon. Why she is so designated is not difficult to ascertain if one knows something about the history of those times. In AD 66 Jewish zealots in Palestine finally instigated a rebellion against Rome, thinking that when a war was started God would be obligated to enter the fray, fight on their side, destroy the enemy, and make them supreme in the world. In AD 70 the Romans finished the war by sacking and burning Jerusalem and the temple. Since the first nation to sack and burn Jerusalem was Babylonia (586 BC), Rome came to be known in Jewish and Christian circles after AD 70 as Babylon (see also 1 Pet 5:13). Thus the harlot is Rome or more precisely the present government of Rome that was persecuting God's people.

If anyone has difficulty with that identification, the author of Revelation removes all doubt in 17:9 and 17:18. In the first of these verses, the author says the seven heads of the beast represent the seven hills on which the woman is seated. Rome was known in antiquity as the city built on seven hills. Further, in 17:18, the author clearly says, "The woman . . . is the great city which has dominion over the kings of the earth." In that time, what city ruled over the "kings of the earth"? The answer—Rome.

One other figure in this chapter must be mentioned. It is found in 17:11: "As for the beast that was and is not, it is an eighth but it belongs to the seven, and it goes to perdition" (i.e., destruction). If one is predisposed to take this passage as a prediction of someone or something to appear in our time, the sky would be the limit for identifying who or what was intended. If, however, one understands the figure in its own time and place, the meaning is clear. The beast in its present "personality" (persecuting the Christians) is no more or no less than Nero come back to life. "It is an eighth, but belongs to the seven." The personality of Nero has come to life again in the Roman Empire under Domitian.

There is nothing esoteric about these passages if one takes time to ascertain what they meant in their own time and place. One thing they definitely are not: predictions of modern-day personalities and events. What does one make of these figures, however, if they are only related to the past? The answer is that the religious truth and principles contained in these writings are just as valid now as they were then. Any time demonic evil takes control and persecutes the people of God and causes great hardship on the earth, then the beast has come alive again and must be resisted by the witness of the faithful. Evil will run its course, but God's intervention will restore sanity to the world. Such occasions arise all too frequently in this world, and when they do, people of lawlessness or sin, antichrists, people of perdition, or whatever their designation arise also.

When one searches the New Testament for the one specific figure that Darbyists are convinced will arise, none is found. In history, evil leaders are without number, unfortunately, and may emerge at any time. Demonic evil does find adherents in this world. Whether there is one specific literal antichrist predicted to come before the return of Jesus is a debatable point. If one argues for such a figure on the basis of 2 Thessalonians 2, it is obvious that no *specific* person is predicted in that passage. And once again, the reader is faced with the problem of making concrete identifications and schemes from literature that is basically symbolic and that was addressed historically to a time and situation already past.

## Note

[1] There is some degree of controversy among New Testament scholars concerning the authorship of 2 Thessalonians. Some argue that Paul wrote the letter, while others believe the book to be pseudonymous, i.e., written by someone else in Paul's name. Since most of the popular writing done during the period 200 BC–AD 100 was done pseudonymously, it is likely that some of the New Testament books fall into that category. For contemporary people, such an act (writing a book or letter under the name of a great church leader, e.g., Paul, Peter, James) would be unthinkable—

immoral, illegal, and unethical. In those days, however, this was a normal practice, and one must understand the books of the New Testament against the backdrop of their own time and place. The point is that some scholars question whether Paul himself actually wrote 2 Thessalonians. Whatever one decides about that issue, the letter is still a part of the inspired canon and is considered revelation for the people of God.

For the purpose of this discussion, there is nothing to be gained by debating the pros and cons of Pauline versus non-Pauline authorship. The passage under question appears to mean essentially the same thing either way. Thus, for this discussion, the author will be cited as Paul, and the reader can understand that designation either way he or she wishes.

## Questions for Study and Discussion

1. What are your beliefs about the antichrist? On what do you base that belief?

2. Do you think the New Testament idea of "antichrist" serves as the basis for popular ideas people hold about that figure today? Why or why not?

3. Why do you believe we have a cultural fascination with the antichrist, such that the figure often appears as a figure in movies and television?

CHAPTER 5

# The Millennium

In addition to the distinction between Israel as the earthly
nation of God and the Christian church as the heavenly kingdom of God, another foundation stone of dispensationalism is
the insistence on the millennial kingdom, a political-type kingdom to be established on earth after Jesus returns. This kingdom
is supposed to be inaugurated at the time of the return of Jesus
(after the church has been removed from the scene and after the
Great Tribulation). Jesus will then sit on the throne of David in
Jerusalem, ruling over an Israelite state for 1,000 years. The dispensationalists are not the only ones who believe in a literal
1,000-year earthly reign of Christ, but the composition of that
kingdom is different among those who are known as premillennial fundamentalists. This interpretation is espoused by those
who presently are intrigued by the *Left Behind* series!

Those who argue the dispensationalist viewpoint with regard
to a literal reign of Jesus on this earth for 1,000 years appeal
strongly to certain prophetic passages they believe must be (1)

taken literally and (2) linked to the 1,000-year period mentioned in Revelation 20. It has already been pointed out that the prophetic passages to which these people appeal are poetic and must be understood poetically. It has also been demonstrated by history itself that the intent and meaning of those prophetic passages have already been fulfilled. The prophets said the Jewish people in Babylonia would be allowed to return home, that a descendant of the Davidic line would sit upon the throne of David, and that the people would become a political state again. All three of these things happened: the Jewish people returned to Palestine in 538 BC; the Davidic descendant, Zerubbabel, sat on the throne as God's "anointed" circa 520–515 BC (granted, this was only for a short time; cf. Hag 2:20-23 and Zech 4:6-10); and the Jewish people became a separate political state in 141 BC, a situation that lasted until 63 BC (but definitely ended by 40–37 BC). There is no unfulfilled prophecy at this point and certainly no mention of any millennium in the Old Testament.

Only one passage in the entire Bible refers to a 1,000-year reign of Jesus with the saints, and this is found in Revelation 20. Again, one is compelled to ask, exactly what does the text say and what does it mean? It is appropriate to examine this important chapter to ascertain what it teaches.

> [1]Then I saw an angel coming down from heaven, holding in his hand the key of the bottomless pit and a great chain. [2]And he seized the dragon, that ancient serpent, who is the Devil and Satan, and bound him for a thousand years, [3]and threw him into the pit, and shut it and sealed it over him, that he should deceive the nations no more, till the thousand years were ended. After that he must be loosed for a little while. [4]Then I saw thrones, and seated on them were those to whom judgment was committed. Also I saw the souls of those who had been beheaded for their testimony to Jesus and for the word of God, and who

had not worshipped the beast or its image and had not received its mark on their foreheads or their hands. They came to life, and reigned with Christ a thousand years. [5]The rest of the dead did not come to life until the thousand years were ended. This is the first resurrection. [6]Blessed and holy is he who shares in the first resurrection! Over such the second death has no power, but they shall be priests of God and of Christ, and they shall reign with him a thousand years. [7]And when the thousand years are ended, Satan will be loosed from prison [8]and will come out to deceive the nations which are at the four corners of the earth, that is, Gog and Magog, to gather them for battle; their number is like the sand of the sea. [9]And they marched up over the broad earth and surrounded the camp of the saints and the beloved city; but fire came down from heaven and consumed them, [10]and the devil who had deceived them was thrown into the lake of fire and sulphur where the beast and the false prophet were, and they will be tormented day and night for ever and ever. [11]Then I saw a great white throne and him who sat upon it; from his presence earth and sky fled away, and no place was found for them. [12]And I saw the dead, great and small, standing before the throne, and books were opened. Also another book was opened, which is the book of life. And the dead were judged by what was written in the books, by what they had done. [13]And the sea gave up the dead in it, Death and Hades gave up the dead in them, and all were judged by what they had done. [14]Then Death and Hades were thrown into the lake of fire. This is the second death, the lake of fire; [15]and if any one's name was not found written in the book of life, he was thrown into the lake of fire.

Before examining this text in some detail, one must be reminded again of the nature of apocalyptic literature—that it consists of a series of visions, each one self-contained. There is little or no real chronological sequence in apocalyptic texts other than descriptions portraying the end of a period of persecution. Another point to keep in mind is that in the English versions of Revelation 20, several misleading translations add to the confusion about how to interpret the chapter correctly.

Perhaps the best way to begin an examination of this passage is to outline the interpretation the Darbyists and their "fellow travelers" use in constructing their ideas about the end times. It is somewhat difficult to do this because the various dispensational groups cannot agree on the exact details, but a general idea of their understandings of this passage can be outlined as follows:

The return of Jesus
Jesus binds Satan
The 1,000-year earthly reign of Jesus
The loosing of Satan
Final battle to end all human history (Armageddon?)
The final judgment (all going to their "reward")

This outline includes only those items that could possibly be understood from the text of this chapter. It may be noted that there is no reference to a rapture or a tribulation, for these ideas have been imported into the scheme.

If one reads the text carefully, one sees that there is no reference to a return of Jesus. A figure comes "down from heaven," but that figure is identified as an "angel," a servant of God. Many will argue that in chapter 19, Jesus has already returned in the figure of the rider on the white horse (19:11-16). It is true that this figure is meant to represent Christ, but there is no reference to a return. This incident in chapter 19 is part of the apocalyptic depiction, which began in chapter 17, of the destruction of the Harlot City (Rome) and the removal of the persecution of Christians in Asia Minor. Jesus as God's agent executes judgment on those who persecute his people. It is not legitimate to shuffle the figures from one section to another. Since chapter 20 begins a new vision (20:1–22:5), a person cannot argue for a return of Jesus from another section, importing it into this passage. (As already noted, the figure in 19:11-16 is not a reference to a return of Jesus anyway.) One therefore looks in vain for any reference in this passage to a return of Jesus.

The second teaching, strongly held, is that Jesus binds Satan for 1,000 years. Again one searches in vain for a reference to Jesus; the angel or servant of God binds Satan. The reference to the 1,000 years is taken literally by the end-times people, since this binding is identified as the same period as the 1,000-year reign of Christ on earth. In apocalyptic literature, numbers are almost always symbolic, and in the book of Revelation up to this point, almost all the numbers have followed the apocalyptic symbolism. Nothing in the text indicates that this understanding of the numbers has changed. The number 10 and its derivatives (i.e., 100, 1,000) denote completeness or inclusiveness in this symbolic scheme. Thus when one reads about 1,000 years in apocalyptic writing, one thinks completeness rather than a literal 1,000 years. It is interesting to note that even if the 1,000 years were to be understood literally, Jesus does not bind Satan and there is no reference to Jesus' return.

The second term of note in this passage concerns the meaning of the binding of Satan. Perhaps the real question here is not the binding but the manner of the binding. The translations are misleading because verse 3 and verse 7 include the phrases "till the thousand years were ended" and "the thousand years are ended." These statements are made in the English translation in the indicative mood, i.e., as if they were facts. The problem is that the Greek text in both instances reads "ended" in the subjunctive mood, i.e., statements made contingently. This means that instead of the end of the binding taking place absolutely in a chronological sequence, the end of the binding takes place modally, contingently. The proper translation of these two passages should read something like "till the thousand years should (would, could) end" and "the thousand years might (could, should) end."

This raises a problem for anyone who sees in this binding a chronological sequence in which Satan is bound, something happens, Satan is released, and then something else occurs. A contingency binding, which is clearly indicated in the Greek text, has an entirely different meaning. To understand this meaning, the interpreter must again look at the context for the writing and the purpose for writing. The Christians in this area were being persecuted because of their loyalty to God and Christ. The rigors of the persecution, however, caused some to waver in their commitment and even to leave the church. The author of Revelation appeals to all Christians to keep the faith, not to become apostate or to go over to the side of the beast. The description of the binding of Satan fits into this drama perfectly.

The binding of Satan is done for 1,000 years, i.e., completely. This important occurrence is accomplished not by Christ but by an angel, a servant of God. When the servants of Christ are dedicated and devoted entirely to Christ and to God's kingdom, Satan is bound, but when these people become apostate and ally themselves with Satan or his representatives, then Satan is loosed, freed to do damage to God's people. In this historical context, people were being asked, in typical apocalyptic thought, to choose between the two, Christ or Satan. When the people choose Christ, Satan is bound; when people choose the beast, then Satan is loosed and the people of God are persecuted. In an apocalyptic time such ideas were common, and one can readily see that the binding of Satan is something that can happen anytime or anywhere a person makes a total commitment to God and God's purposes. A person must be ever vigilant, however, to keep the commitment so that he or she does not violate it either by being deceived or by yielding to the pressures of hard times. This idea is exactly what the author of Revelation tries to communicate to those he addresses.

The next part of the text, and perhaps the most important, concerns the 1,000-year reign of Christ with his people. According to the Darbyists and their "fellow travelers," this will be an earthly kingdom with Jesus ruling over the nation of Israel, sitting on the throne of David in Jerusalem. Others believe this will be a literal 1,000-year earthly kingdom, but they believe the reign of Christ will be with his people (i.e., the church). Some do not hold to any particular place as the center of the kingdom (such as Jerusalem), but they believe the peace of Christ's kingdom will be dominant in the world during this specific period of time. Both of these groups call themselves premillennialists, believing that Jesus will return before (*pre*) the millennial reign.

Mention has already been made of the belief that the church was the millennium and that Jesus would return after (*post*) that period of time. This view is known as postmillennialism. Most in this group believe that the 1,000-year reign has already begun, but there may be a few who think the kingdom will begin later. *After* that period of time (some think of the 1,000 years as literal, others as symbolic), Jesus will return to wrap up all human history and consummate God's kingdom.

There is yet another group known as the a-millennialists (*a* meaning "no"). In this group there are numerous viewpoints, but the basic idea is that these people either do not believe in a millennium at all or do not interpret the 1,000 years in a literal fashion as to time and/or earthly kingdom. As one would imagine, there have been heated debates among the adherents of these three groups. At present, some people still hold to a postmillennial view, but the majority of interpreters today fall into either the premillennial camp or the a-millennial camp. Which is right? An examination of the text itself must determine which, if either, is correct.

Verse 4 depicts a scene in which "those who had been beheaded" for their witness to Christ and God "reigned with Christ a thousand years." There is no mention in this passage of a reformed nation of Israel in Jerusalem. In fact there is no mention of Jerusalem *or the earth* at all! The simple statement is that these martyrs for the cause are reigning with Christ. The logical question is where are Christ and the martyrs?

Throughout the book of Revelation, there are references to Christ and to martyrs. In almost all of the instances (e.g., 5:6-7; 6:9-11), Christ and those who have been faithful to Christ and God are *in heaven*. There is no reason to assume that suddenly they have been transported back to earth, and there is no evidence for that idea in the text. The promise of the entire book has been that those who remain faithful to Christ will not be separated from him by physical death but will be with him wherever he is. In Revelation, Christ resides in heaven. Again the figure of the 1,000 years appears. If it is to be understood symbolically (as it has been throughout the book thus far), it should be understood symbolically here. The saints reigning with Christ for 1,000 years then means that Christ's loyal followers, especially those who have perished in the persecution, are with him completely—perhaps the intended meaning may be *always.*

One may rightly ask exactly what the figure of the millennium means. Again the interpreter must remember that this is apocalyptic literature and that certain characteristics and ideas may appear strange to readers today. Whether these ideas are strange to us is irrelevant since it is the duty of the biblical interpreter to attempt to understand the meaning of the text as it was originally written and understood. In almost every apocalyptic work, one section presents a special reward for those who have kept the faith in the midst of the persecution to the point of laying down their lives for the cause. This special reward is depicted in symbolic language, as one would expect in apocalyptic writings.

Such a reward scene is depicted in Daniel, for example (Dan 12:1-4), and Revelation's description of the 1,000-year reign of Jesus with the martyrs serves exactly the same purpose. One notes again that both of these passages (Dan 12 and Rev 20) are presented in typical apocalyptic ideology and symbolism. As already noted, the group of martyrs are especially singled out (20:4). If one insists on being a literalist, that person must admit that only those who have been "beheaded" can qualify. To insist on such literalism is, however, not necessary or correct when interpreting apocalyptic literature. The author describes a special reward for the martyrs who have lost their lives due to persecution by Rome at that time. Those who are "totally" (1,000) committed to God, Christ, and the kingdom will never be separated from them, and they will reign with Christ (in the heavenly places) always (1,000 years). If one understands this literature and does not read into it schemes about the end times, the meaning is fairly simple to comprehend. (And it is just as true today as it was then.)

There is yet another problem with the *Revised Standard Version* translation (the *King James Version* has it correctly translated). In verses 4-5 there is a reference to resurrection. The proper translation of the Greek here is "lived," not "came to life." The idea of "came to life" places an unfortunate chronological motif in the translated text that is not there in the original writing. All those faithful to Christ, who have been martyred for the cause, will remain with Christ, the relationship unbroken by physical death. The fact that the relationship between the believer and Christ remains unbroken is referred to as the "first resurrection." Those who are in this relationship with God and Christ need not fear the "second death." The "first death"" is obviously physical death, which everyone must experience.

Though the time and means of physical death may be tragic (in this context, martyr death), the fact of physical death holds no fear for the faithful. The most important death, the death to be feared, is called the "second death." This second death is not defined until a bit later; verse 14 denotes the ultimate separation from God based on whether individuals responded positively to God's offer of grace and new life and remained faithful in the face of persecution.

The reference to Satan's being loosed in verses 7-9 indicates that God's people endured persecution at that time. It is interesting to note that there is no reference in the passage to Armageddon, and neither is a battle fought. Many have been led to believe that at this point in the chronology of the end times, *the* great battle to end all human history will occur. Such is not the case. Neither here nor in 16:16 (where Armageddon is mentioned) is a battle fought. God intervenes directly and does away with the persecution. Some of the more recent interpretations from the Darbyist tradition have altered the ideas connected with Armageddon. Because Armageddon is not found in chapter 20 of Revelation but in 16:16, for "chronological" reasons these advocates now speak about Armageddon as a war (sometimes extended) rather than a battle. If there is no battle described in connected with Armageddon, how could there possibly be an extended war?

Closely related to these ideas is the interpretation proposed for "Gog and Magog." Several identifications have been postulated for these two enigmatic terms. One of the most popular, especially a few years ago (and still persisting in slightly different forms), was to view one of them as Russia and the other as Red China.

To understand what Gog and Magog means, one must return to the book of Ezekiel where the phrase originally appeared (Ezek 38–39). In the ministry of the prophet Ezekiel, who spoke during the period of the Babylonian captivity, the return of the Jewish exiles to Palestine and Jerusalem was predicted. Before that could happen, however, the persecutors of God's people had to be destroyed or removed from the scene. They were designated by Ezekiel as Gog and Magog and were used in Ezekiel to refer to the period of Babylonian captivity. The persecutor at that time was Babylon. The terms Gog and Magog then originally referred to Babylon, but as the reader of Revelation has learned there is a new Babylon. The new Babylon is Rome, the agency persecuting the people of God at that time. So again there is no esoteric prediction of modern times, only a description, using a symbolic figure from Ezekiel, of what was happening when Revelation was written.

Up to this point in Revelation 20, there is no reference to a return of Jesus, no reference to Jesus binding Satan, no reference to an earthly political state, no earthly reign of Jesus on the throne of David in Jerusalem, no chronological sequence of events, no mention of the great battle (or war) of Armageddon and in fact no mention of any battle at all, no prediction of modern (i.e., twenty-first century) nations, and no prediction of the end of human history. Naturally, there is no mention of any rapture or Great Tribulation; these have had to be violently "imported" into the text. There is no mention of "double" comings of Jesus or of two periods of three and a half years each. In short, almost the entire Darbyist scheme of what happens at the end time, rooted in Revelation 20, is simply not there.

The only item that is in the text is a depiction of the "final judgment," and that is done in symbolic imagery. The popular interpretation of this passage (20:11-15) is that there will be a great gathering of all the dead at one time. It is true that the judgment is depicted as the final judgment for the dead, but there is no compelling evidence here to demand that this all happens at one moment. What the passage teaches is that *all* people must stand before the judgment seat of God and be responsible for what they have done. At first glance this may seem to give the idea of a "works righteousness" where God keeps a log, adds up a person's good deeds, and subtracts the bad deeds. If the ledger is tilted to one side, that determines the reward or punishment of the person.

The text does not seem to teach that kind of salvation, however. The book of life is the author's way of indicating that God's grace and mercy are prior to anything a human being can do with regard to salvation. Throughout the book of Revelation, the people of God are urged to remain faithful to God and Christ, and the others are urged to repent and become a part of the people of God. "What they had done," therefore, in this passage relates to whether the people of God remained loyal in the time of persecution and whether others had responded positively to the revelation given through the witness of the church. It could be that the author of Revelation has in mind here a final judgment on one momentous occasion, but there is every reason to think that he is simply emphasizing that all people will ultimately have to face God's judgment.

One of the primary reasons for doubting that the author conceived of a last great judgment is that there is no evidence in the passage or in the entire book of Revelation, properly understood, that the author expected human history to come to a close. One finds a description in 21:1–22:5 of a new age, but this is a transformed period of human history with the persecution of God's people gone. The reference in 21:1, "and the sea was no more," means the source of the persecution is now gone (one recalls that the beast that persecuted God's people in chapter 13 rose out of the sea). Further, one reads that the new Jerusalem, which is described in marvelous terms, comes down out of heaven to earth (cf. 21:2-3, 10-11). God's dwelling is with the human race (21:3, 22).

To illustrate that all human history has not come to a conclusion with all going to their reward (either heaven or hell), the author speaks of nations still existing (21:24, 26; 22:2) and the continuing work of the people of God, to take God's healing revelation to the world (22:2). This particular feature of the "chronology" has caused many to question the order of the text here. For those who understand the nature of apocalyptic writings, that it is not primarily concerned with chronology, there is no real problem. The meaning of the text is clear enough. If one wishes to impose literalism on the text, however, there is a problem. For example, there are two descents of the New Jerusalem to the earth in chapter 21 (verses 2-3 and verses 10-11). Unless there is something wrong with the author or unless there are two New Jerusalems, the interpreter must understand that these are two symbolic representations of the same idea.

The simple truth is that the book of Revelation does not predict the end of the world or the return of Jesus, even though for many years people have understood it in that light. If it was originally intended to do so, the author was woefully wrong in his understandings. The fact is that this great apocalyptic work was written, as almost all apocalyptic works, to bolster the faith of the people of God in a time of persecution. The author urged them to hold fast to the faith even if it meant deprivation or perhaps death. That the book was written for those people in that time is clearly shown by the continuing promises that the end (i.e., of the persecution) was coming soon. God through his agent the Christ would remove the persecution and allow the people of God to worship and live again as they should. This was to happen soon. One finds the words "soon" or "near" in the introduction (1:1-3) and "soon" four times and "near" once in the epilogue (22:6-21), which also includes a short section indicating that all this activity was to take place shortly (22:10-11). It would have been of no comfort at all to these people undergoing persecution in AD 90–95 to learn that almost 1,900 years later, their sufferings would be over!

Further, the idea of a millennial kingdom *on earth* is simply not in the text of Revelation. If one wishes to believe that such is going to occur, that is fine as long as one does not force the idea onto the biblical text. And if someone wishes to believe in raptures and tribulations and reestablished kingdoms of ancient Israel and antichrists and all the rest, that is fine too. But one must be honest with the intent and meaning of the biblical texts. To force ideas onto and into them is to do violence to God's inspired word. Schemes and scenarios that try to depict the end of history and the return of Jesus are interesting, sometimes exciting, but all of them belong under the category of fiction. The truth here is that the New Testament writers do not give us any accounts detailing the end of the world. They believed the future belongs to God to work out as God determines. Idle speculation, ingenious schemes, forced interpretations, and the identification of biblical symbols with specific people and events now may stimulate excitement, but such activities are simply a matter of playing games with the sacred texts.

## Questions for Study and Discussion

1. Do you think there could be a "perfect" kingdom in this world?

2. Do you believe that God's people who remain faithful will receive a special reward? Why or why not?

3. Can God's people aggressively pursue the call to make disciples of all nations in a period of persecution? If not, how do they witness to their faith?

4. Are there ever times in which the church should actively and aggressively try to make "disciples of all nations"? Why or why not?

5. What is your belief about the 1,000-year reign of Jesus on Earth? On what do you base this belief?

CHAPTER 6

# Observations about the End Times according to Biblical Teachings

It is appealing and comforting for people to believe they are in possession of knowledge others do not have. This is especially true in matters of religion generally but in particular when that knowledge concerns the end of the world and the future, what it holds, what is going to happen, and how and when. It is perhaps natural for people to be curious about the future, but that curiosity becomes dangerous when schemes about the end of the world are devised and biblical texts are used as authority for them. There is much discussion on such matters and numerous schemes about end times are current in our generation. Whenever one reads or hears about one of these schemes, however, the proper question must always be this: Are these theories true to the biblical texts?

As some of the more sophisticated dispensationalists have correctly argued, the relative newness of a system, the origin of its proponents, and the question of whether the theory has been divisive in the church should have no place in determining the rightness or wrongness of the system. It is quite fair, however, to examine origins and personalities and consequences of the teaching to ascertain what presuppositions and circumstances were attendant to the shaping of the ideas and the interpretation of the texts and to determine what types of people have been attracted to these schemes. The primary consideration of any theological or religious teaching set forth as biblical is that the teaching actually be in accordance with the intention and meaning of the original text as it was presented by the inspired author(s) to the people of God.

There is no need at this point to rehearse the teachings claimed by the dispensationalists for the absolute separation and distinction between the church and Israel, for the ideas about rapture, the Great Tribulation, the antichrist, the millennium, and the end of all human history (especially that which is read into the book of Revelation). These matters have already been discussed, and the bottom line is that the biblical texts, understood in context against the historical setting of their own times and properly as literary form, do not teach the ideas claimed by the advocates of the Darbyist system.

If such people were a small minority, one could dismiss them and their system as simply nonsense. These people, however, have become increasingly zealous in their quest to disseminate their teachings, and in many churches the membership is polarized between those who are Darbyists and those who are not. In fact, several mainline Protestant denominations at one time or another have either officially or unofficially determined that the dispensational system is heresy! For example, in the late 1930s and early 1940s the Presbyterian Church in the United States wrestled with this issue. A committee of the

General Assembly was formed to study the dispensational system and bring a report on that teaching. This was done in 1944. The committee was asked to study "the Question as to whether the Type of Biblical Interpretation Known as Dispensationalism Is in Harmony with the Confession of Faith."

The report of the committee to the General Assembly came to the following conclusion: "It is the unanimous opinion of your Committee that Dispensationalism as defined and set forth above is out of accord with the system of doctrine set forth in the Confession of Faith." To help that decision reach the membership of the churches, the following statement was included in the "Report on Study Committee on Religious Education and Publication": "IV. That the Executive Committee make available to the churches of the Assembly in pamphlet form the report of the Ad Interim Committee 'On Changes in Confession of Faith and Catechisms' (Dispensationalism); adopted at this Assembly."

Subsequent to this discussion, Dr. Lewis Sperry Chafer, one of the leading dispensational theologians, protested the decision of the 1944 assembly. In 1945 at the next General Assembly, his protest was considered. The decision of the 1945 assembly reaffirmed that of the 1944 assembly—. "The Assembly is unable to see that Dr. Chafer's teachings have been misinterpreted. It is therefore unwilling to rescind the statement or suppress the literature containing the same."[4] No stand was taken on the idea of a premillennial return of Jesus, however.

Obviously, many have either forgotten or have never known about this action of the Presbyterian (U.S.) General Assembly taken in 1944. In fact, this church as such no longer exists since it merged in 1983 with the United Presbyterian Church in the U.S.A. to form the Presbyterian Church (U.S.A.). Perhaps it is time for all church bodies to study this teaching again and to educate the membership about it, because the Darbyist system is

being aggressively taught and church people are being taken in
by the sincere but incorrect teaching. This is especially true
today with the popularity of the *Left Behind* books.

Even more disturbing is the fact that this type of teaching is
vigorously pushed among young people who are not equipped
to make proper value judgments about the validity of such ideas.
The most disturbing aspect of all, however, is the fact that this
type of teaching and some of its components have entered into
modern twenty-first-century politics. The most obvious example
is the zeal for the creation and sustaining support of the modern
state of Israel. To the Darbyists, this new state, which emerged
in 1948, was a "fulfillment of prophecy." The event was cele-
brated among this group because it meant the rapture, the
return of Jesus, and the millennial kingdom were near. Of
course, there is to be a Great Tribulation also, but the Darbyists
believe they will not participate in it since the rapture will get
them out of the world before the suffering begins (at least the
pre-tribulationists).

Coupled with this idea was also the teaching that the rapture
and the beginning of the end times would come in 1988. The
way this date was calculated is interesting. Using several texts
from the Old Testament prophets that speak of the Jewish
people returning home (from Babylon in 538, *not* in 1948), the
idea developed that there would be a generation between the
actual return to Palestine and the beginning of the new age (cf.
Jer 30–31; Ezek 36–39). The reasoning was that since Israel
became a political state in 1948, a generation (i.e., forty years)
after that would yield 1988. It is interesting to note that some of
the prognosticators even then were already "hedging their bets,"
probably so they would not be embarrassed again by missing the
time (as had happened so often in the past). Their argument was
that a generation today is longer than in biblical times, lasting
about seventy years. Therefore, while these people set the tenta-
tive date of 1988 as the beginning of the end times, there was an

option out on 2018. After that year comes and goes, I fearlessly predict that other dates will be suggested.

When such ideas and schemes are combined with the political processes in this world and when divine assent and direction are claimed for these ideas, situations can be (and have been) highly explosive and dangerous. One may believe, for example, that it was right and just for the state of Israel to be created in 1948. One must not, however, misuse the biblical writings to support its creation. The phenomenon of Zionism was a twentieth-century political movement with no biblical basis except that its adherents and other exponents misused the texts to argue for divine sanction for their actions. This is not to argue for or against the creation of the state of Israel or its legitimacy or its right to exist. It is to make clear that the Scripture itself has nothing to say about it.

Further, it is scary when people, claiming the authority of Scripture, begin to talk about the *inevitability* of a nuclear war that will kill billions of people because of a description in the Bible (Rev 8:8-9, e.g.). It is certainly possible that the human race will in its madness resort to nuclear war that will kill billions of people, but it will happen because of the depravity of the human race and not because it is predicted in the Bible. To talk about the *possibility* of such a holocaust is one thing; to talk about its *inevitability* is another. So much of the talk about Armageddon (understood as a battle, or a war as some now argue) focuses on the nearness of the event. A political figure who may be susceptible to such ideology may feel that it would be better to get on with it than to delay it further. Such an action would then become a self-fulfilling prophecy, one that was predicted and then manipulated into happening. The claim could then be made that the prophecy was true and happened as predicted. Such reasoning is circular at best, nonsensical when viewed against the biblical texts and their original meaning, and extremely dangerous and deadly at worst.

In the past, religious zealots with wild ideas, sincerity, and blind faith have wreaked havoc on peoples and nations because they have provoked actions by people who were also sincere and misled by these zealots. To cite only one example, during the first century AD the Roman state ruled over Palestine. The Jewish people chafed under that rule, and frequently during that time zealot leaders and groups arose advocating open war with Rome. The reasoning was based partially on some of the same prophetic texts Darbyists use today and partially on a sincere but wrong belief that if a war could be started with Rome, God would be honor-bound to intervene on their behalf and destroy the hated Romans. The idea was that the sooner the war was started, the sooner God would be forced into action. Finally, in AD 66 the war was begun. In September, AD 70, the Romans sacked and burned Jerusalem, a victory that is still commemorated (from the Roman perspective) in the Triumphal Arch of Titus where the central feature is the menorah (the seven-pronged candle stand representing the Jewish people). Learning how to understand and interpret the biblical texts properly is a necessity for truly religious people; sometimes it is a matter of life or death!

In the past, apocalyptic literature was a strange and mysterious part of the biblical writings. Since the key to understanding this literature and thought pattern was lost after circa AD 100, most of the interpreters in the church gave lip service to it without truly knowing what it was about. Naturally, people from early times until now have attempted to use these writings and ideas to make schemes and timetables for the end of the world. Though all have been wrong, this does not seem to deter the "faithful" who put their trust in the end-time events. It would appear that after so many incidents in which the people who "cipher out" such matters are wrong, it would dawn on thinking people that these texts did not and were not intended to give some esoteric account of the end times. Yet people are still being misled.

Because the key to understanding apocalyptic writing has been rediscovered in recent times through the location and study of apocalyptic books, it is time for ministers and educators in churches to begin to teach the correct understanding of this type of literature. That area has been left open to the sensationalists far too long. The fact that so many church people have heard the Darbyist interpretation and believed it should not deter us from the task of making this part of Scripture clear and meaningful to the church again. Revelation, for example, is too powerful and beautiful a book to be left to the sensationalists, no matter how dedicated and sincere they may be.

The process of reeducating people away from Darbyism will not be an easy task, because so many people have grounded their entire Christian theology and faith-security in this type of interpretation and understanding of the biblical texts. Challenging such interpretations causes an emotional response because those asked to put aside these ideas and learn the correct interpretation feel that the new interpretation is a direct threat to the security of faith. This is partly due to the fact that so many (though not all) of the Darbyists either imply or state that anyone who does not agree with their interpretation is a liberal, an atheist, or an apostate who has joined Satan and the beast. One of the favorite ploys at this point is for the Darbyists to quote Revelation 22:18-19: "I warn every one who hears the words of the prophecy of this book: if any one adds to them, God will add to him the plagues described in this book, and if any one takes away from the words of this prophecy, God will take away his share in the tree of life and the holy city, which are described in this book."

Such "oaths" were common in apocalyptic writings to give added hope to the people undergoing persecution at that time. The message of apocalyptic is that God ultimately takes away the persecution and that the persecuted people can count on it. This passage was not intended as a threat of divine punishment for anyone who does not agree with a particular interpretation of Scripture.

Because of such emotional reactions both from the teachers of this system and from its devotees, many pastors have simply left the matter alone. However, it is past time when we can do this. Too many young people are being deceived by these teachings, too many people have their faith misplaced because of these teachings, and too many groups with political power are full of these ideas. It can be, and indeed is, dangerous to sit idly by and continue to allow improper interpretations of Scripture to upset people's lives and perhaps be politically destructive.

The bottom line lies in the proper interpretation of Scripture. To understand what the biblical writers meant, one must place oneself, insofar as possible, in the same time, place, and culture as the original writer and hearers. Only when this is done can the ideas and principles taught in these books be properly ascertained. If the interpreter comes to these writings with a different set of presuppositions, as the Darbyists undoubtedly do, there is no chance to interpret the text as originally written. The basic structure of the books has been altered, and no amount of quoting and weaving the biblical passages can make the new system biblical.

Our examination of the key passages used as a foundation for the ideas about Israel, rapture, antichrist, Great Tribulation, and millennium has shown that none of these passages teach what the Darbyists claim. There is no basis for the strict distinction between Israel as a Jewish state and the Christian church unless one already believes that this is what the texts are saying. The rapture, however one may wish to interpret that idea, does not mean what the Darbyists claim; for them it is only a convenient device to rid the world of the church so that God can start the prophetic time clock again to deal with the world through a political Israel. Typical apocalyptic teaching suggests a period of intense persecution of the people of God each time evil gains the upper hand. Whether such an occasion will arise at the "last day" is not clear in the New Testament, given the symbolic nature of the texts as well as their specific historical settings. Further, there is almost no evidence for a predicted figure called "antichrist" to come in the future, and the idea of a millennial kingdom here on *earth* is simply not in Revelation 20, the only place that figure is used in the entire Scripture.

Couple these uncertainties and nonexistent ideas with the dispensationalist and fundamentalist methodology of drawing verses and parts of verses from all over the Bible irrespective of the meaning of these texts within their larger contexts, and one has a situation that produces dramatic reading. It is totally fiction, however. If someone wishes to believe the Darbyist schemes, that is one thing. If one wants to claim biblical support for them, that is an entirely different matter. It is past time to call this system of interpretation what it really is: unbiblical and nonsensical.

Since this system, or parts of this system, is all that many people in the church have ever heard about these matters, the question must be raised concerning what the Bible really does teach about the "end times." It is clear that the New Testament writers do comment on these matters, but they do not always speak with a unified voice. It is time for pastors to take up the study of some of these controversial passages and discuss them with their congregations. It is time for laity to examine the biblical texts for themselves to ascertain what they really say instead of swallowing the fantastic schemes of the Darbyists.

There is, of course, in the New Testament a clear belief that the final victory belongs to God. How that victory will be specifically accomplished, or when, or under what circumstances, is *not* taught in these books. The sooner we can trust God to bring end times about when and where and how God wishes, the sooner we can get on with more important matters, namely the carrying out of our elective purpose, witnessing to the power of the new life loosed by God in the resurrection of Jesus. We can get on with allowing that power to transform our lives and through us, it is hoped, the lives of others, in order to make our society and the world reflect the unsearchable riches of Christ.

## Notes

[1] This report can be found in its entirety in the *Minutes of the Eighty-Fourth General Assembly of the Presbyterian Church in the United States* (Austin: Von Boeckmann-Jones Co., 1944), 123-27.

[2] Ibid., 126.

[3] Ibid., 82.

[4] *Minutes*, 1945, 65.

## Questions for Study and Discussion

1. Do you think there have been times in the past when people have used interpretations of Scripture to support questionable causes?

2. How should modern political states and leaders be guided by the principles set forth in Scripture?

3. How can we who live in an era so distant from biblical times apply the principles of Scripture?

4. What do you think the New Testament says about the return of Jesus?

5. What level of importance do you place on having a belief about the end times?

6. Should your church library or media center stock copies of dispensationalist fiction like *Left Behind*? Why or why not?

# EPILOGUE

To many people, the foregoing discussion may seem strange since the Darbyist/Fundamentalist interpretations of the rapture, antichrist, and millennium are so widely known and vigorously held by a large number of people in our culture today. To find that in the Scripture itself there is no mention of the rapture, an antichrist, or a millennial kingdom here on earth is a shock to many and an outrage to others! Most of us have been led to believe that the Scripture, especially the books of Daniel and Revelation, contain mystical secrets that, if properly understood, would yield a clue and even a detailed step-by-step account to the mysteries about the return of Jesus and the end of the world. This has been so much a part of our heritage that it is unthinkable to believe anything else about these writings. The simple fact, however, is that there is no mention of any of these ideas especially as they have been popularly propounded by those who espouse "end-times" doctrines.

What the Scriptures do teach to God's people, especially those under persecution even to the point of death, is that God is ultimately the final arbiter in these matters. What is important is for God's people to remain loyal to the faith in spite of anything that might arise in this fallen world so permeated with sin and evil.

There are great depths of religious insight in the Scriptures that become obscured when we read them as a road map for the end of the world. The New Testament teaches that God's purposes will ultimately be done in God's creation, but much of this is taught in symbolic language and even in hyperbole. This is especially true with the book of Revelation, the central theme of which is the supreme majesty and power of God. This concept is seen primarily in the visions and in the scenes of multitudes raising their voices as one in hymns of praise and honor to the One who sits upon the throne and to His Lamb, slain but standing with complete power and wisdom.

There are other themes as well, namely that of God's justice and righteousness. It is made clear that God's judgment will surely come upon evil in whatever form it appears. Some people, when they read Revelation or other apocalyptic works, are a bit uneasy, for the writings themselves cry out for the judgment of God to fall upon the evil of the world. Some perceive a great distance between this idea and Jesus' "Father, forgive them." Yet there is a place for this kind of cry because the biblical writers all emphasized the serious consequences of rejecting God's laws, love, and offers of redemption and forgiveness. Surely if there is any justice in the world and if the God we worship is righteous and just, there must be an appropriate verdict on hideous evil. One example would, of course, be the attempt of the Nazis to exterminate the Jews before and during World War II. If indeed God's righteousness does not ultimately prevail and such evil does not receive its just deserts, then all of life is a farce, a travesty of law, a jungle in which might makes right and the law of power and might always prevails in spite of moral considerations. There is a place in God's plan for judgment of our world, but it is to executed by God through whatever means God chooses.

Another point bothers some, especially those who are anxious for the "end" to come. If there is a place for judgment, why is it delayed? Why do God's people especially have to endure persecution and suffering? Several biblical writers seem to answer that God stays the judgment because of God's love. God loves all creatures and beings and desires that all have ample time and opportunity to repent. The cry of the martyrs— "How long?"—is answered with a command for patience. It is not that God does not love those who have been faithful to death, but God loves the others also. God's patience and love for sinners led to the gift of God's Son and the death of that Son. The followers of Jesus cannot expect less than the same treatment Jesus received. But the great hope is that this suffering can be vicarious, that is, that it can lead sinners to an acceptance of the new life God has made available to everyone. Therefore, the "end" has been delayed as the later New Testament writers came to understand (see especially Matt 24–25 and 2 Pet 3), but the final victory will belong to God and to those who have been faithful. What God's people are supposed to do in the "interim" is what they were originally called to do—make the revelation of this God known to all people as the Great Commission challenged.

The biblical writers seem concerned with two points: (1) evil is to be judged by God, and (2) God's people have a special standing with God, but it is more a calling to perform than "goodies" to glean while others pay their "dues." Our task is to proclaim God's good news and cease trying to figure out schemes, codes, and wild scenarios pertaining to Jesus' return and the end of the world. This is something we must leave to God; it is God's business and not ours. We are not doing well at fulfilling our responsibilities, let alone trying to run God's business! As the great prophet Isaiah challenged the people of Israel in times long ago, "Trust God." And he made it clear to them that if they would not trust God, they would not be established.

# BIBLIOGRAPHY AND OTHER SUGGESTED READINGS

Numerous books by many authors deal with the Darbyist interpretation of the biblical books, especially Daniel and Revelation.
Listed here are only a few representing the various viewpoints.
The reader will find additional bibliographic listings in the
books cited here.

## The History of Darbyism

Kraus, C. Norman. *Dispensationalism in America.* Richmond: John
Knox Press, 1958.

Marsden, George M. *Fundamentalism and American Culture: The
Shaping of Twentieth Century Evangelicalism: 1870–1925.*
Oxford: Oxford University Press, 1980.

———. *Reforming Fundamentalism: Fuller Seminary and the New
Evangelicalism.* Grand Rapids: Eerdmans, 1987.

———. *Understanding Fundamentalism and Evangelicalism.*
Eerdmans, 1991.

Rowdon, Harold H. *The Origins of the Brethren, 1825–1850.*
London: Pickering & Inglis, 1967.

Sandeen, Ernest R. *The Roots of Fundamentalism: British and
American Millenarianism,* Chicago: University of Chicago Press,
1970.

Williams, Michael. *This World Is Not My Home: The Origins and Development of Dispensationalism.* Christian Focus Publications, 2003.

## Darbyist Interpretation

Baker, Charles F. *A Dispensational Theology.* Grand Rapids MI: Grace Bible College Publications, 1971.

Hitchcock, Mark and Thomas Ice. *The Truth Behind Left Behind: A Biblical View of the End Times.* Sisters OR: Multnomah, 2004.

LaHaye, Tim, and Thomas Ice. *Charting the End Times: A Visual Guide to Bible Prophecy & Its Fulfillment.* Harvest House, 2001.

———. *The End Times Controversy: The Second Coming Under Attack.* Eugene OR: Harvest House, 2003.

LaHaye, Tim, and Jerry B. Jenkins. *Are We Living in the End Times?* Wheaton IL: Tyndale House, 2000.

———, and Chris Fabry. *A Kid's Guide to Understanding the End Times.* Harvest House, 2004.

Lindsey, Hal, with C. C. Carlson. *The Late Great Planet Earth.* Grand Rapids: Zondervan Publishing House, 1971.

———. *The Rapture: Truth or Consequences.* New York: Bantam Books, 1983.

Ryrie, Charles C. *Dispensationalism Today.* Chicago: Moody Press, 1965.

———. *Dispensationalism* (revised and expanded edition). Chicago: Moody Publishers, 1995.

———. *What You Should Know About the Rapture.* Chicago: Moody Press, 1981.

Showers, Renald. *There Really Is a Difference!: A Comparison of Covenant and Dispensational Theology.* Bellmawr NJ: Friends of Israel, 1990.

Walvoord, John F. *The Blessed Hope and the Tribulation.* Grand Rapids: Zondervan, 1976.

———. *The Millennial Kingdom: A Basic Text in Premillennial Theology.* Zondervan, 1983.

————. *The Prophecy Knowledge Handbook*. Wheaton IL: Victor Books, 1990.


## Progressive Dispensationalism

Bateman, Herbert W. *Three Central Issues in Contemporary Dispensationalism: A Comparison of Traditional and Progressive Views*. Grand Rapids: Kregel, 1999.

Blaising, Craig A. and Darrell L. Bock, editors. *Dispensationalism, Israel and the Church: The Search for Definition*. Grand Rapids: Zondervan, 1992.

————. *Progressive Dispensationalism*. Baker Academic, 2000.

Saucy, Robert L. *The Case for Progressive Dispensationalism*. Grand Rapids: Zondervan, 1993.


## Novels from a Darbyist Perspective

LaHaye, Tim, and Jerry B. Jenkins. *Left Behind Series*. Tyndale House.

1: *Left Behind*, 1995
2: *Tribulation Force*, 1996
3: *Nicolae*, 1997
4: *Soul Harvest*, 1998
5: *Apollyon*, 1999
6: *Assassins*, 1999
7: *The Indwelling*, 2000
8: *The Mark*, 2000
9: *Desecration*, 2001
10: *The Remnant*, 2002
11: *Armageddon*, 2003
12: *Glorious Appearing*, 2004

————. *Countdown to the Rapture Series*. Tyndale House.
1: *The Rising*, 2005 (additional titles forthcoming)

## Films & Videos from a Darbyist Perspective

*Left Behind: The Movie.* Vision Video (2000).
*Left Behind II: Tribulation Force.* Vision Video (2002).
*Left Behind: World at War.* Vision Video (2005).
*Vanished in the Twinkling of an Eye.* Cloud Ten Pictures (2000).

## Multiple Views in One Book

Bock, Darrell L. *Three Views on the Millennium and Beyond.* Grand
    Rapids: Zondervan, 1999.
Gundry, Stanley L. *Three Views on the Rapture.* Zondervan, 1996.
Pate, C. Marvin. *Four Views on the Book of Revelation.* Zondervan,
    1998.

## Darbyism and Eschatology from Other Perspectives

Allis, O.T. *Prophecy and the Church.* Philadelphia: Presbyterian &
    Reformed Publishing Co., 1945.
Bass, Clarence B. *Backgrounds to Dispensationalism: Its Historical
    Genesis and Ecclesiastical Implications.* Grand Rapids: Wm. B.
    Eerdmans Publishing Co., 1960.
Beegle, Dewey M. *Prophecy and Prediction.* Ann Arbor.: Pryor
    Pettengill, 1978.
DeMar, Gary. *End Times Fiction.* Nashville: Thomas Nelson
    Publishers, 2001.
Forbes, Bruce David and Jeanne Halgren Kilde, eds. *Rapture,
    Revelation and the End Times: Exploring the Left Behind Series.*
    Macmillan, 2004.
Frykholm, Amy Johnson. *Rapture Culture: Left Behind in Evangelical
    America.* Oxford: Oxford University Press, 2004.
Fuller, Daniel P. "The Hermeneutics of Dispensationalism." Th.D.
    diss., Northern Baptist Theological Seminary, 1966.
Gerstner, John H. *Wrongly Dividing The Word of Truth: A Critique of
    Dispensationalism* (2d edition). Soli Deo Gloria, 2000.

Gundry, Robert H. *The Church and the Tribulation.* Grand Rapids: Grand Rapids: Zondervan Publishing House, 1973.

Hoekman, Anthony A. *The Bible and the Future.* Grand Rapids: Wm. B. Eerdmans Publishing Co., 1979.

Poythress, Vern. *Understanding Dispensationalists.* Phillipsburg, PA: P & R Publishing, 1993.

Rossing, Barbara. *The Rapture Exposed.* Boulder CO: Westview Press, 2005.

## Books and Commentaries to Assist in Proper Interpretation of Daniel and Revelation

Beasley-Murray, G. R. *The Book of Revelation.* Grand Rapids: Wm. B. Eerdmans Publishing Co., 1981.

Caird, G. B. *A Commentary on the Revelation of St. John the Divine.* New York: Harper & Row, 1966.

Dawn, Marva J. *Joy in Our Weakness: A Gift of Hope From the Book of Revelation* (revised edition). Grand Rapids: Eerdmans, 2002.

Efird, James M. *Daniel and Revelation: A Study of Two Extraordinary Visions.* Eugene OR: Wipf & Stock Publishers, 2001.

———. *How to Interpret the Bible.* Eugene OR: Wipf & Stock Publishers, 2000.

———. *Revelation for Today: An Apocalyptic Approach.* Nashville: Abingdon Press, 1989.

Goldingay, John E. *Daniel: Word Biblical Commentary.* Nashville: Word Publishing, 1987.

Gowan, Donald E. *Daniel: Abingdon Old Testament Commentaries.* Nashville: Abingdon Press, 2001.

Hill, Craig C. *In God's Time: The Bible and the Future.* Grand Rapids: Eerdmans, 2002.

Keener, Craig S. *Revelation: The NIV Application Commentary.* Grand Rapids: Zondervan, 2000.

Koester, Craig R. *Revelation and the End of All Things.* Grand Rapids: Eerdmans, 2001.

Lucas, Ernest C. *Daniel: Apollos Old Testament Commentary.* Downers Grove IL: InterVarsity, 2002.

McConville, J. Gordon. *Exploring the Old Testament: A Guide to the Prophets*. Volume 4. Downers Grove IL: InterVarsity, 2002.

Parvin, Samuel F. and Stephen Byrum. *Unlocking the Mysteries: 150 FAQs About Revelation and the End of the World*. Nashville: Abingdon Press, 1999.

Porteous, Norman. *Daniel: A Commentary*. Philadelphia: Westminster Press, 1965.

Reddish, Mitchell. *Revelation*: Smyth & Helwys Bible Commentary. Macon: Smyth & Helwys, 2001.

Smith-Christopher, Daniel L. *The Book of Daniel* in volume 7 of *The New Interpreter's Bible*. Nashville: Abingdon Press, 1996.

Towner, Sibley. *Daniel*. Edited by James L. Mays and Patrick D. Miller. Atlanta: John Knox Press, 1984.

Wainwright, Arthur W. *Mysterious Apocalypse: Interpreting the Book of Revelation*. Nashville: Abingdon Press, 1993. (Now available through Henrickson Publishers.)

Witherington, Ben. *Revelation: The New Cambridge Bible Commentary*. Cambridge: Cambridge University Press, 2003.